THIRD EDITION

INTRO A

Skills for Success
LISTENING AND SPEAKING

Kevin McClure | Mari Vargo

OXFORD
UNIVERSITY PRESS

OXFORD
UNIVERSITY PRESS

198 Madison Avenue
New York, NY 10016 USA

Great Clarendon Street, Oxford, OX2 6DP, United Kingdom

Oxford University Press is a department of the University of Oxford.
It furthers the University's objective of excellence in research, scholarship,
and education by publishing worldwide. Oxford is a registered trade
mark of Oxford University Press in the UK and in certain other countries

ISBN: 978 0 19 490488 9   STUDENT BOOK INTRO A WITH IQ ONLINE PACK
ISBN: 978 0 19 490476 6   STUDENT BOOK INTRO A AS PACK COMPONENT
ISBN: 978 0 19 490536 7   IQ ONLINE STUDENT WEBSITE

Printed in China

This book is printed on paper from certified and well-managed sources

ACKNOWLEDGEMENTS

Back cover photograph: Oxford University Press building/David Fisher

Illustrations by: emc design p. 80; 5W Infographics p. 93, p. 96.

*The Publishers would like to thank the following for their kind permission to
reproduce photographs and other copyright material*:

123rf: pp. 5 (hiker in mountains/maridav), 42 (berries/PaylessImages),
43 (meat/niloo138), (vegetables/foodandmore), (fruit/Giuseppe Elio
Cammarata), 44 (donuts/belchonock), 48 (milk/serezniy), 50 (market stall/
satina), 51 (salad/zazastudio), 53 (chilies/Natalia Klenova), 116 (fast food/
dolgachov), 133 (kayakers/langstrup); **Alamy:** pp. 10 (looking out of car
window/CSI Productions), 22 (student recreation room/Raul J Garcia), 30
(dorm room/Glasshouse Images), 33 (university library/PvE), 34 (fencing/
Stephen Shepherd), 43 (desserts/Pavel Kibenko), 48 (ingredients list/
FoodIngredients), 51 (eggs on toast/David Lee), 60 (shopping mall/__David
Gee), 63 (man reading book/Tetra Images), 64 (woman with umbrella/
Cultura Creative), (crowded city street/Alvey & Towers Picture Library), 72
(woman in scarf/Mint Images Limited), 75 (rollercoaster/Blaine Harrington
III), 85 (modern apartments/andrew parker), 86 (apartments to rent/
incamerastock), 88 (aerial view of settlement/mauritius images GmbH),
91 (swimming pool/Andreas von Einsiedel), (fireplace/Image Source
Plus), 102 (laughing bike shop assistant/Rimagine Group Limited), 112
(soccer player training/Tony Tallec), 113 (two students studying/Antonio
Guillem Fernández), 119 (two mountain bikers/Cultura Creative), 123
(rice terraces/Elena Ermakova), 125 (people crossing in Manhattan/
Littleny), (temple in Ubud/Peter Schickert), (canal in Bruges/kavalenkava
volha), 129 (young female traveler/Mariusz Szczawinski), 132 (fruit stall
in Dhaka/Maciej Dakowicz), 135 (architect/Tetra Images, LLC), 138 (Grand
Bazaar in Istanbul/Izel Photography), 139 (hand holding shells/Leszek
Czerwonka), 140 (Acropolis in Athens/nick baylis), 141 (Trafalgar square/
JOHN KELLERMAN), (British museum/Loop Images Ltd), (Globe theatre/
Ian Dagnall), 148 (girl in phone shop/Juice Images), 157 (Muslim bride
and groom/özkan özmen), 159 (boy on phone/Vadym Drobot), 161 (laptop/
Oleksiy Maksymenko Photography), 162 (train station ticket office/
Holmes Garden Photos); **Getty:** pp. cover (purple sequins on fabric/
Philippe Intraligi/EyeEm), 2 (painting mural/Cavan Images), 4 (young
group hiking forest/Hero Images), 5 (man playing soccer/Pornsawan
Sangmanee/EyeEm), (choir/Maskot), (woman cooking/mapodile), (men
playing game/10'000 Hours), 6 (baking cookies/ielanum), 9 (teacher
and children on fieldtrip/Hero Images), 11 (businessman on bike/Cavan
Images), 13 (painter/portishead1), 14 (scrabble/Science & Society Picture
Library), 17 (surfer/David Pu'u), 21 (young people collecting litter/
South_agency), 26 (woman waving at laptop/FatCamera), 31 (students
walking to school/Matt Henry Gunther), 37 (students in food hall/Frédéric
Soltan), 39 (college campus/HaizhanZheng), 40 (boats laden with food/
Wahyu Noviansyah/EyeEm), 45 (woman eating strawberries/andresr), 47
(family preparing to eat/PeopleImages), 57 (woman laughing /subman),
58 (beekeeper tending bees/Ian Lishman), 61 (family playing board game/
vgajic), 65 (young women on hiking trip/Tomas Rodriguez), 66 (young
men doing judo/Jun Tsukuda/Aflo), 70 (men jogging on road/Kaewmanee
Saekang/EyeEm), 71 (two friends playing basketball/Christopher Malcolm),
72 (man pondering/kupicoo), 76 (small house/Mireya Acierto), 78 (beach
front apartments/Arterra), 97 (Lofoten Islands/Roberto Moiola/Sysaworld),
98 (running club at sunrise/SolStock), 100 (tired woman/elenaleonova),
103 (family having breakfast/eli_asenova), 106 (pills spilled from bottles/
anilakkus), 111 (yoga teacher/Dean Mitchell), 120 (Kuala Lumpur/seng
chye teo), 128 (Museo Soumaya/Matt Mawson), 130 (woman in gallery/JGI/
Tom Grill), 135 (public speaker/Hero Images), 143 (student at Taj Mahal/
swissmediavision), 144 (sports crowd/simonkr), 152 (businessman on
laptop/Westend61), 153 (frustrated businessman/Jose Luis Pelaez Inc), 154
(frustrated woman with phone/JGI/Jamie Grill), 159 (frustrated woman
with laptop/Maskot), 163 (family relaxing in house/Maskot); **OUP:** pp. 5
(male tennis player/Shutterstock/VGstockstudio), 24 (university campus
in fall/Shutterstock/Jorge Salcedo), 51 (fast food/Shutterstock/Studio
37), 66 (skier/Shutterstock/Samot), 67 (potter making pot/Shutterstock/
MarinaGrigorivna), 68 (chairs on beach/Shutterstock/Sarah Jane Taylor),
(kite/Shutterstock/stable), (motorcycle/123rf/Bogdan Ionescu), 141 (Tower
of London/Shutterstock/donsimon); **Shutterstock:** pp. 15 (washing
car/Nomad_Soul), 28 (man taking notes/fizkes), 43 (dairy products/
bitt24), (whole grains/Tamakhin Mykhailo), 79 (city apartment building/
Sean Pavone), 90 (car in driveway/Imagenet), 104 (working and eating/
fizkes), 107 (taking vitamin pills/goffkein.pro), 109 (healthy salad bowl/
AnikonaAnn), 114 (man working late/mavo), 124 (Roman forum ruins/
Nejron Photo), 147 (old cellphone/Ayah Raushan), 161 (smartphone/
OSABEE), (smartwatch/BallBall14); **Third party:** pp. 89 (Jack Sparrow
house/Jonathan Melville-Smith), 156 (Esplorio app logo/Esplorio).

ACKNOWLEDGMENTS

We would like to acknowledge the teachers from all over the world who participated in the development process and review of *Q: Skills for Success* Third Edition.

USA

Kate Austin, Avila University, MO; **Sydney Bassett**, Auburn Global University, AL; **Michael Beamer**, USC, CA; **Renae Betten**, CBU, CA; **Pepper Boyer**, Auburn Global University, AL; **Marina Broeder**, Mission College, CA; **Thomas Brynmore**, Auburn Global University, AL; **Britta Burton**, Mission College, CA; **Kathleen Castello**, Mission College, CA; **Teresa Cheung**, North Shore Community College, MA; **Shantall Colebrooke**, Auburn Global University, AL; **Kyle Cooper**, Troy University, AL; **Elizabeth Cox**, Auburn Global University, AL; **Ashley Ekers**, Auburn Global University, AL; **Rhonda Farley**, Los Rios Community College, CA; **Marcus Frame**, Troy University, AL; **Lora Glaser**, Mission College, CA; **Hala Hamka**, Henry Ford College, MI; **Shelley A. Harrington**, Henry Ford College, MI; **Barrett J. Heusch**, Troy University, AL; **Beth Hill**, St. Charles Community College, MO; **Patty Jones**, Troy University, AL; **Tom Justice**, North Shore Community College, MA; **Robert Klein**, Troy University, AL; **Patrick Maestas**, Auburn Global University, AL; **Elizabeth Merchant**, Auburn Global University, AL; **Rosemary Miketa**, Henry Ford College, MI; **Myo Myint**, Mission College, CA; **Lance Noe**, Troy University, AL; **Irene Pannatier**, Auburn Global University, AL; **Annie Percy**, Troy University, AL; **Erin Robinson**, Troy University, AL; **Juliane Rosner**, Mission College, CA; **Mary Stevens**, North Shore Community College, MA; **Pamela Stewart**, Henry Ford College, MI; **Karen Tucker**, Georgia Tech, GA; **Loreley Wheeler**, North Shore Community College, MA; **Amanda Wilcox**, Auburn Global University, AL; **Heiko Williams**, Auburn Global University, AL

Canada

Angelika Brunel, Collège Ahuntsic, QC; **David Butler**, English Language Institute, BC; **Paul Edwards**, Kwantlen Polytechnic University, BC; **Cody Hawver**, University of British Columbia, BC; **Olivera Jovovic**, Kwantlen Polytechnic University, BC; **Tami Moffatt**, University of British Columbia, BC; **Dana Pynn**, Vancouver Island University, BC

Latin America

Georgette Barreda, SENATI, Peru; **Claudia Cecilia Díaz Romero**, Colegio América, Mexico; **Jeferson Ferro**, Uninter, Brazil; **Mayda Hernández**, English Center, Mexico; **Jose Ixtaccihuastl**, Instituto Tecnológico de Tecomatlán, Mexico; **Andreas Paulus Pabst**, CBA Idiomas, Brazil; **Amanda Carla Pas**, Instituição de Ensino Santa Izildinha, Brazil; **Allen Quesada Pacheco**, University of Costa Rica, Costa Rica; **Rolando Sánchez**, Escuela Normal de Tecámac, Mexico; **Luis Vasquez**, CESNO, Mexico

Asia

Asami Atsuko, Jissen Women's University, Japan; **Rene Bouchard**, Chinzei Keiai Gakuen, Japan; **Francis Brannen**, Sangmyung University, South Korea; **Haeyun Cho**, Sogang University, South Korea; **Daniel Craig**, Sangmyung University, South Korea; **Thomas Cuming**, Royal Melbourne Institute of Technology, Vietnam; **Nguyen Duc Dat**, OISP, Vietnam; **Wayne Devitte**, Tokai University, Japan; **James D. Dunn**, Tokai University, Japan; **Fergus Hann**, Tokai University, Japan; **Michael Hood**, Nihon University College of Commerce, Japan; **Hideyuki Kashimoto**, Shijonawate High School, Japan; **David Kennedy**, Nihon University, Japan; **Anna Youngna Kim**, Sogang University, South Korea; **Jae Phil Kim**, Sogang University, South Korea; **Jaganathan Krishnasamy**, GB Academy, Malaysia; **Peter Laver**, Incheon National University, South Korea; **Hung Hoang Le**, Ho Chi Minh City University of Technology, Vietnam; **Hyon Sook Lee**, Sogang University, South Korea; **Ji-seon Lee**, Iruda English Institute, South Korea; **Joo Young Lee**, Sogang University, South Korea; **Phung Tu Luc**, Ho Chi Minh City University of Technology, Vietnam; **Richard Mansbridge**, Hoa Sen University, Vietnam; **Kahoko Matsumoto**, Tokai University, Japan; **Elizabeth May**, Sangmyung University, South Korea; **Naoyuki Naganuma**, Tokai University, Japan; **Hiroko Nishikage**, Taisho University, Japan; **Yongjun Park**, Sangji University, South Korea; **Paul Rogers**, Dongguk University, South Korea; **Scott Schafer**, Inha University, South Korea; **Michael Schvaudner**, Tokai University, Japan; **Brendan Smith**, RMIT University, School of Languages and English, Vietnam; **Peter Snashall**, Huachiew Chalermprakiet University, Thailand; **Makoto Takeda**, Sendai Third Senior High School, Japan; **Peter Talley**, Mahidol University, Faculty of ICT, Thailand; **Byron Thigpen**, Sogang University, South Korea; **Junko Yamaai**, Tokai University, Japan; **Junji Yamada**, Taisho University, Japan; **Sayoko Yamashita**, Jissen Women's University, Japan; **Masami Yukimori**, Taisho University, Japan

Middle East and North Africa

Sajjad Ahmad, Taibah University, Saudi Arabia; **Basma Alansari**, Taibah University, Saudi Arabia; **Marwa Al-ashqar**, Taibah University, Saudi Arabia; **Dr. Rashid Al-Khawaldeh**, Taibah University, Saudi Arabia; **Mohamed Almohamed**, Taibah University, Saudi Arabia; **Dr. Musaad Alrahaili**, Taibah University, Saudi Arabia; **Hala Al Sammar**, Kuwait University, Kuwait; **Ahmed Alshammari**, Taibah University, Saudi Arabia; **Ahmed Alshamy**, Taibah University, Saudi Arabia; **Doniazad sultan AlShraideh**, Taibah University, Saudi Arabia; **Sahar Amer**, Taibah University, Saudi Arabia; **Nabeela Azam**, Taibah University, Saudi Arabia; **Hassan Bashir**, Edex, Saudi Arabia; **Rachel Batchilder**, College of the North Atlantic, Qatar; **Nicole Cuddie**, Community College of Qatar, Qatar; **Mahdi Duris**, King Saud University, Saudi Arabia; **Ahmed Ege**, Institute of Public Administration, Saudi Arabia; **Magda Fadle**, Victoria College, Egypt; **Mohammed Hassan**, Taibah University, Saudi Arabia; **Tom Hodgson**, Community College of Qatar, Qatar; **Ayub Agbar Khan**, Taibah University, Saudi Arabia; **Cynthia Le Joncour**, Taibah University, Saudi Arabia; **Ruari Alexander MacLeod**, Community College of Qatar, Qatar; **Nasir Mahmood**, Taibah University, Saudi Arabia; **Duria Salih Mahmoud**, Taibah University, Saudi Arabia; **Ameera McKoy**, Taibah University, Saudi Arabia; **Chaker Mhamdi**, Buraimi University College, Oman; **Baraa Shiekh Mohamed**, Community College of Qatar, Qatar; **Abduleelah Mohammed**, Taibah University, Saudi Arabia; **Shumaila Nasir**, Taibah University, Saudi Arabia; **Kevin Onwordi**, Taibah University, Saudi Arabia; **Dr. Navid Rahmani**, Community College of Qatar, Qatar; **Dr. Sabah Salman Sabbah**, Community College of Qatar, Qatar; **Salih**, Taibah University, Saudi Arabia; **Verna Santos-Nafrada**, King Saud University, Saudi Arabia; **Gamal Abdelfattah Shehata**, Taibah University, Saudi Arabia; **Ron Stefan**, Institute of Public Administration, Saudi Arabia; **Dr. Saad Torki**, Imam Abdulrahman Bin Faisal University, Dammam, Saudi Arabia; **Silvia Yafai**, Applied Technology High School/Secondary Technical School, UAE; **Mahmood Zar**, Taibah University, Saudi Arabia; **Thouraya Zheni**, Taibah University, Saudi Arabia

Turkey

Sema Babacan, Istanbul Medipol University; **Bilge Çöllüoğlu Yakar**, Bilkent University; **Liana Corniel**, Koc University; **Savas Geylanioglu**, Izmir Bahcesehir Science and Technology College; **Öznur Güler**, Giresun University; **Selen Bilginer Halefoğlu**, Maltepe University; **Ahmet Konukoğlu**, Hasan Kalyoncu University; **Mehmet Salih Yoğun**, Gaziantep Hasan Kalyoncu University; **Fatih Yücel**, Beykent University

Europe

Amina Al Hashamia, University of Exeter, UK; **Irina Gerasimova**, Saint-Petersburg Mining University, Russia; **Jodi**, Las Dominicas, Spain; **Marina Khanykova**, School 179, Russia; **Oksana Postnikova**, Lingua Practica, Russia; **Nina Vasilchenko**, Soho-Bridge Language School, Russia

CRITICAL THINKING

The unique critical thinking approach of the *Q: Skills for Success* series has been further enhanced in the Third Edition. New features help you analyze, synthesize, and develop your ideas.

Unit question

The thought-provoking unit questions engage you with the topic and provide a critical thinking framework for the unit.

UNIT QUESTION

How do you use technology?

A. Discuss these questions with your classmates.

1. Look at the photo. What kind of technology do you see?
2. How do you think these people are using the technology?
3. How do you use this type of technology?

Analysis

You can discuss your opinion of each listening text and analyze how it changes your perspective on the unit question.

SAY WHAT YOU THINK

SYNTHESIZE Think about Listening 1, Listening 2, and the unit video as you discuss the questions.

1. How do you feel when you forget your cell phone? Why?
2. Do you think cell phones make life easier or harder? Explain.
3. Imagine that nobody has a cell phone. How is your life different? Think of five examples.

CRITICAL THINKING STRATEGY

Relating to ideas

To **relate** to an idea is to connect yourself to it. Relating to an idea helps you understand it better. When you learn about a new idea, think about your opinions about it or how it might affect you.

iQ PRACTICE Go online to watch the Critical Thinking Video and check your comprehension. *Practice > Unit 6 > Activity 9*

NEW! Critical Thinking Strategy with video

Each unit includes a Critical Thinking Strategy with activities to give you step-by-step guidance in critical analysis of texts. An accompanying instructional video (available on iQ Online) provides extra support and examples.

E. CATEGORIZE Read the meal descriptions in Activity D again. How are they similar to or different from your diet? Take notes in the chart. Then rank the diets from 1 (most similar to yours) to 4 (least similar to yours). Share with a partner.

Others' diets	Similarities to my diet	Differences from my diet	Ranking
1. Nour			
2. Alex			
3. Cynthia			
4. Pedro			

NEW! Bloom's Taxonomy

Blue activity headings integrate verbs from Bloom's Taxonomy to help you see how each activity develops critical thinking skills.

F. CREATE Write answers to the questions.

1. What do you usually eat for breakfast, lunch, and dinner?

2. Do you think you have a balanced diet? Explain.

3. Based on your answers to questions 1 and 2, do you think you should take supplements? Why or why not?

THREE TYPES OF VIDEO

UNIT VIDEO

The unit videos include high-interest documentaries and reports on a wide variety of subjects, all linked to the unit topic and question.

NEW! "Work with the Video" pages guide you in watching, understanding, and discussing the unit videos. The activities help you see the connection to the Unit Question and the other texts in the unit.

CRITICAL THINKING VIDEO

NEW! Narrated by the *Q* series authors, these short videos give you further instruction on the Critical Thinking Strategy of each unit using engaging images and graphics. You can use them to gain a deeper understanding of the Critical Thinking Strategy.

SKILLS VIDEO

NEW! These instructional videos provide illustrated explanations of skills and grammar points in the Student Book. They can be viewed in class or assigned for a flipped classroom, for homework, or for review. One skill video is available for every unit.

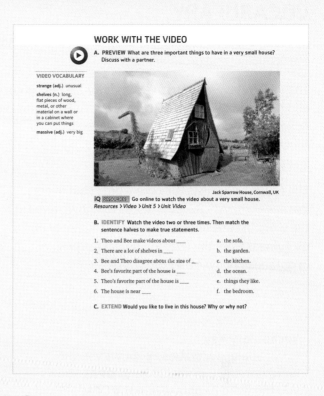

WORK WITH THE VIDEO

A. PREVIEW What are three important things to have in a very small house? Discuss with a partner.

VIDEO VOCABULARY

strange (adj.) unusual

shelves (n.) long, flat pieces of wood, metal, or other material on a wall or in a cabinet where you can put things

massive (adj.) very big

Jack Sparrow House, Cornwall, UK

iQ RESOURCES Go online to watch the video about a very small house. *Resources > Video > Unit 5 > Unit Video*

B. IDENTIFY Watch the video two or three times. Then match the sentence halves to make true statements.

1. Theo and Bee make videos about ___
2. There are a lot of shelves in ___
3. Bee and Theo disagree about the size of ___
4. Bee's favorite part of the house is ___
5. Theo's favorite part of the house is ___
6. The house is near ___

a. the sofa.
b. the garden.
c. the kitchen.
d. the ocean.
e. things they like.
f. the bedroom.

C. EXTEND Would you like to live in this house? Why or why not?

💡 How to compare and contrast

Venn Diagram

Firefighter — Both — Police Officer

fights fires — *help people* — *fights crime*

stays at the station until called — *have dangerous jobs* — *works on the street*

Easily access all videos in the Resources section of iQ Online.

VOCABULARY

A research-based vocabulary program focuses on the words you need to know academically and professionally.

The vocabulary syllabus in *Q: Skills for Success* is correlated to the CEFR (see page 76) and linked to two word lists: the Oxford 3000 and the OPAL (Oxford Phrasal Academic Lexicon).

⚑ OXFORD 3000

The Oxford 3000 lists the core words that every learner at the A1– B2 level needs to know. Items in the word list are selected for their frequency and usefulness from the Oxford English Corpus (a database of over 2 billion words).

> **Vocabulary Key**
> In vocabulary activities, ⚑ shows you the word is in the Oxford 3000 and **OPAL** shows you the word or phrase is in the OPAL.

PREVIEW THE LISTENING

A. VOCABULARY Here are some words from Listening 2. Read the definitions. Then complete the sentences below.

affordable *(adjective)* not expensive
condition *(noun)* ⚑ OPAL something in good condition is not damaged or broken
demand *(noun)* ⚑ OPAL a need or want
entertainment *(noun)* ⚑ fun or free-time activities
housing *(noun)* ⚑ apartments, houses, and homes
increase *(verb)* ⚑ OPAL to become bigger
landlord *(noun)* a person—he or she rents homes to people for money
shortage *(noun)* not enough of something

⚑ Oxford 3000™ words   OPAL Oxford Phrasal Academic Lexicon

OPAL
OXFORD PHRASAL ACADEMIC LEXICON

NEW! The OPAL is a collection of four word lists that provide an essential guide to the most important words and phrases to know for academic English. The word lists are based on the Oxford Corpus of Academic English and the British Academic Spoken English corpus. The OPAL includes both spoken and written academic English and both individual words and longer phrases.

Academic Language tips in the Student Book give information about how words and phrases from the OPAL are used and offer help with features such as collocations and phrases.

ACADEMIC LANGUAGE
You can use *available* with or without the preposition *to* after it. You can use different verbs before *available*: *be available*, *become available*, *make* (something) *available*.

_____ **OPAL**
Oxford Phrasal Academic Lexicon

1. I couldn't go online with my old cell phone. It wa[s]
   a. You can go online with a smartphone.
   b. You can't go online with a smartphone.
2. The new cell phone is not <u>available</u> to buyers yet. [...] next Monday.
   a. You can buy the new cell phone now.
   b. You can't buy the new cell phone now.
3. Eric is <u>working on</u> his paper. It's due on Wednesd[ay]
   a. Eric is at work.
   b. Eric is writing his paper.
4. I can send you <u>text messages</u> while I'm at work, b[ut]
   a. A text message is the same thing as a phone ca[ll]
   b. A text message is not the same thing as a phon[e]
5. Margo <u>keeps in touch</u> with her old friends. She li[kes] they're doing.
   a. When you keep in touch with someone, you se[e]
   b. When you keep in touch with someone, you d[on't]

EXTENSIVE READING

NEW! Extensive Reading is a program of reading for pleasure at a level that matches your language ability.

There are many benefits to Extensive Reading:

- It helps you to become a better reader in general.
- It helps to increase your reading speed.
- It can improve your reading comprehension.
- It increases your vocabulary range.
- It can help you improve your grammar and writing skills.
- It's great for motivation to read something that is interesting for its own sake.

Each unit of *Q: Skills for Success* Third Edition has been aligned to an Oxford Graded Reader based on the appropriate topic and level of language proficiency. The first chapter of each recommended graded reader can be downloaded from iQ Online Resources.

UNIT 1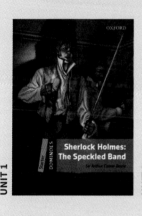

UNIT 2

UNIT 3

UNIT 4

UNIT 5

UNIT 6

UNIT 7

UNIT 8

iQ ONLINE extends your learning beyond the classroom.

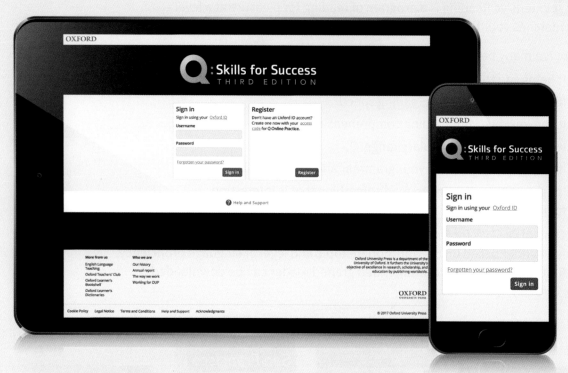

- Practice activities provide essential skills practice and support.
- Automatic grading and progress reports show you what you have mastered and where you need more practice.
- The Discussion Board allows you to discuss the Unit Questions and helps you develop your critical thinking.
- Essential resources such as audio and video are easy to access anytime.

NEW TO THE THIRD EDITION

- iQ Online is optimized for mobile use so you can use it on your phone.
- An updated interface allows easy navigation around the activities, tests, resources, and scores.
- New Critical Thinking Videos expand on the Critical Thinking Strategies in the Student Book.
- The Extensive Reading program helps you improve your vocabulary and reading skills.

How to use iQ ONLINE

Go to **Practice** to find additional practice and support to complement your learning in the classroom.

Go to **Resources** to find:
- All Student Book video
- All Student Book audio
- Critical Thinking videos
- Skills videos
- Extensive Reading

Go to **Messages** and **Discussion Board** to communicate with your teacher and classmates.

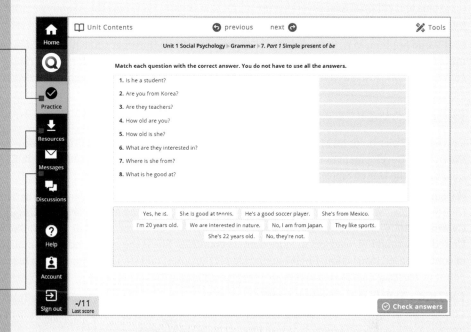

A progress bar shows you how many activities you have completed.

View your scores for all activities.

Online tests assigned by your teacher help you assess your progress and see where you need more practice.

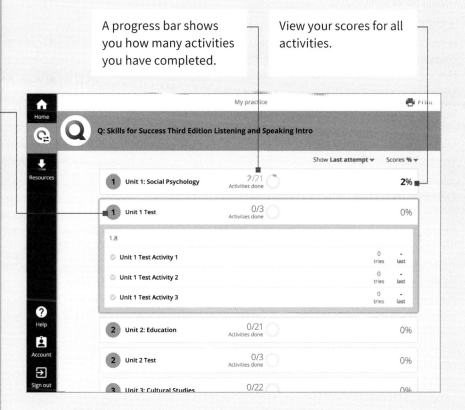

AUTHORS AND CONSULTANTS

AUTHORS

Kevin McClure holds an M.A. in Applied Linguistics from the University of South Florida and has taught English in the United States, China, France, and Japan. In addition to his extensive teaching experience, he has managed language programs and editorial teams working on online courseware. He is now the AI and Assessment Lead for DynEd International in San José, California. He is currently developing and refining intelligent assessments.

Mari Vargo holds an M.A. in English from San Francisco State University. She has taught numerous ESL courses at the university level. She has also written textbooks and online course materials for a wide range of programs, including community colleges, universities, corporations, and primary and secondary schools.

SERIES CONSULTANTS

Lawrence J. Zwier holds an M.A. in TESL from the University of Minnesota. He is currently the Associate Director for Curriculum Development at the English Language Center at Michigan State University in East Lansing. He has taught ESL/EFL in the United States, Saudi Arabia, Malaysia, Japan, and Singapore.

Marguerite Ann Snow holds a Ph.D. in Applied Linguistics from UCLA. She teaches in the TESOL M.A. program in the Charter College of Education at California State University, Los Angeles. She was a Fulbright scholar in Hong Kong and Cyprus. In 2006, she received the President's Distinguished Professor award at CSULA. She has trained ESL teachers in the United States and EFL teachers in more than 25 countries. She is the author/editor of numerous publications in the areas of content-based instruction, English for academic purposes, and standards for English teaching and learning. She is a co-editor of *Teaching English as a Second or Foreign Language* (4th ed.).

CRITICAL THINKING CONSULTANT James Dunn is a Junior Associate Professor at Tokai University and the Coordinator of the JALT Critical Thinking Special Interest Group. His research interests include critical thinking skills' impact on student brain function during English learning as measured by EEG. His educational goals are to help students understand that they are capable of more than they might think and to expand their cultural competence with critical thinking and higher-order thinking skills.

ASSESSMENT CONSULTANT Elaine Boyd has worked in assessment for over 30 years for international testing organizations. She has designed and delivered courses in assessment literacy and is also the author of several EL exam coursebooks for leading publishers. She is an Associate Tutor (M.A. TESOL/Linguistics) at University College, London. Her research interests are classroom assessment, issues in managing feedback, and intercultural competences.

VOCABULARY CONSULTANT Cheryl Boyd Zimmerman is Professor Emeritus at California State University, Fullerton. She specialized in second-language vocabulary acquisition, an area in which she is widely published. She taught graduate courses on second-language acquisition, culture, vocabulary, and the fundamentals of TESOL, and has been a frequent invited speaker on topics related to vocabulary teaching and learning. She is the author of *Word Knowledge: A Vocabulary Teacher's Handbook* and Series Director of *Inside Reading, Inside Writing*, and *Inside Listening and Speaking*, published by Oxford University Press.

ONLINE INTEGRATION Chantal Hemmi holds an Ed.D. TEFL and is a Japan-based teacher trainer and curriculum designer. Since leaving her position as Academic Director of the British Council in Tokyo, she has been teaching at the Center for Language Education and Research at Sophia University in an EAP/CLIL program offered for undergraduates. She delivers lectures and teacher trainings throughout Japan, Indonesia, and Malaysia.

COMMUNICATIVE GRAMMAR CONSULTANT Nancy Schoenfeld holds an M.A. in TESOL from Biola University in La Mirada, California, and has been an English language instructor since 2000. She has taught ESL in California and Hawaii, and EFL in Thailand and Kuwait. She has also trained teachers in the United States and Indonesia. Her interests include teaching vocabulary, extensive reading, and student motivation. She is currently an English Language Instructor at Kuwait University.

CONTENTS

Social Psychology

CRITICAL THINKING	noticing similarities
VOCABULARY	collocations for hobbies and interests
GRAMMAR	simple present of *be*; simple present of other verbs
PRONUNCIATION	simple present third-person *-s*/*-es*
SPEAKING	keeping a conversation going
NOTE-TAKING	writing important words

What are you interested in?

A. Discuss these questions with your classmates.

1. What do you talk about with a new friend? Circle the topics. Add one topic.

music	photos you see online
sports	family
movies	work
books	_____
videos you see online	

2. What activities do you like?

3. Look at the photo. What is this person doing? Are you interested in this activity?

B. Listen to *The Q Classroom* online. Then answer these questions.

1. What did the students say? What are they interested in?

2. Do the students like the same things you like?

iQ PRACTICE   Go to the online discussion board to discuss the Unit Question with your classmates. *Practice > Unit 1 > Activity 1*

UNIT OBJECTIVE

Listen to a radio program. Use information and ideas to interview a classmate. Then introduce him or her to the class.

3

LISTENING

OBJECTIVE ▶

Are You Interested in Hiking?

You are going to listen to a radio discussion at a school. Think about what interests you.

PREVIEW THE LISTENING

A. VOCABULARY Here are some words and phrases from the listening. Read the definitions. Then circle the correct word or phrase to complete each conversation.

ACADEMIC LANGUAGE

Interested is one of the most common academic words. *Interested in* is a common spoken phrase. Speakers often use the phrase at the beginning of a lesson to focus on a topic.

_____ **OPAL**
Oxford Phrasal Academic Lexicon

كلمات وتعبيرات

> **belong to** *(verb phrase)* 🔑 to be a member of a group
>
> **club** *(noun)* 🔑 a group of people—they meet and do things together
>
> **collect** *(verb)* 🔑 to get and keep many things because you like them
>
> **good at** *(phrase)* 🔑 can do something well
>
> **hobbies** *(noun)* 🔑 activities—you do them for fun
>
> **interested in** *(phrase)* 🔑 OPAL enjoying an activity or a topic
>
> **team** *(noun)* 🔑 a group of people—they play a sport or a game together

🔑 Oxford 3000 keywords   **OPAL** Oxford Phrasal Academic Lexicon

1. A: Do you (collect /(belong to)) the math club?

   B: Yes, I do. We meet on Thursdays.

2. A: I like basketball, but I can't play it well.

   B: My roommate is very ((good at)/ team) basketball. He can teach you.

3. A: Wow, you're a great soccer player! Are you on the soccer (hobbies /(team))?

   B: Thanks! Yes, I am.

4. A: What do you like to do?

   B: Oh, I have a lot of (interested in / (hobbies)). I play tennis, I go hiking, and I like poetry.

5. A: Is there a book (team / (club)) at this school?

   B: Yes, there is. We meet in the library every Wednesday night. It's fun!

6. A: You have a lot of postcards!

   B: I (hobbies / (collect)) them. I have more than 2,000 postcards.

7. A: I like the museum. Are you (belong to / (interested in)) history?

   B: Yes. History is my favorite class.

iQ PRACTICE Go online for more practice with the vocabulary.
Practice › Unit 1 › Activities 2–3

B. CATEGORIZE Read the sentences. Write *T* (true) or *F* (false). Then correct the false statements. Compare your answers with a partner.

_T_ 1. I collect coins. *I collect coins*

_F_ 2. I belong to a book club. *I don't belong*

_T_ 3. I am interested in sports. *I am don't interested in sports*

_T_ 4. I am good at writing. *I like to travel*

_T_ 5. My hobbies are soccer and cooking. *I like to cooking*

C. PREVIEW You are going to listen to a radio discussion. The speakers talk about hobbies, or things they like to do. Look at the photos. Match the hobby with the photo.

_3_ cooking   _5_ hiking   _2_ singing
_1_ soccer   _4_ tennis   _6_ video games

WORK WITH THE LISTENING

A. CATEGORIZE Read the sentences. Then listen to the discussion. Write *T* (true), *F* (false), or *N* (not enough information).

iQ RESOURCES Go online to download extra vocabulary support.
Resources > Extra Vocabulary > Unit 1

F 1. All the speakers are students.

F 2. All the speakers have hobbies.

F 3. All the speakers play sports.

T 4. Some of the speakers belong to clubs.

T 5. Some of the speakers are new students.

B. IDENTIFY Listen again. What are the people interested in? Check (✓) the correct activities.

	Sara	Hiro	Daniel	Ben	Mei
clubs	✓	☐	✓	☐	✓
teams	☐	✓	✓	☐	☐
hiking	✓	☐	☐	☐	☐
music	✓	☐	☐	✓	☐
soccer	☐	✓	☐	✓	☐
photography	☐	✓	☐	☐	✓
tennis	☐	☐	✓	☐	☐
math	☐	☐	✓	☐	☐
video games	☐	☐	☐	✓	☐
baking/cooking	☐	✓	✓	☐	☐
getting together with friends on weekends	☐	✓	✓	✓	✓

baking cookies

 CRITICAL THINKING STRATEGY

Noticing similarities

When you hear information about different things or people, some information may be the same or similar.

- Listen for words that show things that are the same.

- You can also listen for words that are different but have the same, or a similar, meaning. These words are called **synonyms**.

Noticing similarities can help you group or categorize the information you hear.

Information	Similarities
Anita in interested in music and <u>art</u>. Hugo is interested in <u>art</u> and sports.	Both Anita and Hugo are interested in art.
Cara enjoys <u>hiking</u>. Steven likes <u>walking outdoors</u> and <u>climbing mountains</u>.	Both Cara and Steven enjoy hiking. (Hiking is a type of walking outdoors. These words are synonyms.)
Michael plays <u>tennis</u> and <u>baseball</u>. Lucy plays <u>basketball</u>. Xander is on the <u>soccer</u> team.	Michael, Lucy, and Xander all play sports: tennis, baseball, basketball, and soccer.

iQ PRACTICE Go online to watch the Critical Thinking Video and check your comprehension. *Practice > Unit 1 > Activity 4*

C. INVESTIGATE Interview three or more of your classmates about how they feel today. Take notes. Try to notice similarities in their responses and report back to the class.

D. ANALYZE Look at the chart in Activity B. Complete the sentences about similarities. Then compare your answers with a partner.

1. _____, _____, and _____ belong to clubs.

2. _____ and _____ are on a soccer team.

3. _____ and _____ are interested in photography.

4. _____ and _____ like to bake or cook.

5. _____, _____, _____, and _____ get together with friends on weekends.

E. CREATE Look at the chart in Activity B again. Answer the questions.

1. Which person is the most similar to you? _____

2. How are you and that person similar? What things do you do that are the same?

   _____

3. Are you similar to any of the other speakers? If so, who else are you similar to and how? _____

   _____

F. IDENTIFY Listen again. Circle the correct answer.

1. Mei's last name is ____.

   a. Lee   b. Cheng   c. Thien

2. Sara ____ with a group.

   a. sings   b. plays music   c. runs

3. Hiro reads ____.

   a. the newspaper   b. books on history   c. video game
      every day   magazines

4. Daniel is good at ____.

   a. history   b. music   c. math

5. Ben likes to collect ____.

   a. baseball hats   b. postcards   c. pens

iQ PRACTICE Go online for additional listening and comprehension.
Practice > Unit 1 > Activity 5

BUILDING VOCABULARY Collocations for hobbies and interests

Some words usually go together. These are called **collocations**.

Verb (phrase) + preposition + noun	Verb + noun
be good at volleyball / math	**go** shopping / hiking
be interested in books / sports	**play** sports / tennis / games
be on a team	**read** books / magazines
belong to a book club	**ride** a bicycle / a bike
get together with friends	**take** lessons
go to a museum / the beach / a park	**watch** a movie / television (TV)
listen to the radio	
live in Tokyo	

🔊 **A. APPLY** Complete the collocations with words from the box above.
Then listen to check your answers.

Alan lives <u>*live in Tokyo*</u> Toronto. He works at the after-school program
            1

at the community center in his town. Children come to the community

center after school. Alan does many activities with them. It's a good job for

him because he is interested ___<u>*friends*</u>___ a lot of different things.
                                  2

He is good <u>*play sports*</u> sports. On sunny days, Alan and the kids
             3

_____ride_____ bikes or ____go____ hiking. Sometimes they
4   5

go ___to___ the beach or the park. On rainy days, Alan and the
6

kids __watch__ movies, or they ____Play____ games like
7   8

Scrabble and checkers. Sometimes they ____go____ to a museum
9

together. After work, Alan sometimes gets __together__ with friends,
10

but he usually goes home to relax and ____read____ a book.
11

B. RESTATE Listen to the people talk about themselves. Write two sentences
about each speaker. Use the words in parentheses.

1. **Saud** (reads) _____

   (is interested in) _____

2. **Khalid** (plays) _____

   (rides) _____

C. CREATE Write three sentences about you. Use collocations from the box
on page 8.

1. _____

2. _____

3. _____

iQ PRACTICE Go online for more practice with collocations for hobbies and
interests. *Practice > Unit 1 > Activity 6*

WORK WITH THE VIDEO

A. PREVIEW How do you get around your town or city? What kinds of transportation do you take?

VIDEO VOCABULARY

crazy (adj.) not based on reason, experience, or good judgment

tail (n.) the back part of a plane

come out (v. phr.) to reach or stretch over an area

vehicle (n.) a thing that is used for transporting people or things from one place to another

go crazy / go nuts (v. phr.) to become very enthusiastic or excited about something

show up (v. phr.) to arrive

iQ RESOURCES Go online to watch the video about someone's hobby.
Resources > Video > Unit 1 > Unit Video

B. ANALYZE Watch the video two or three times. Take notes in the first part of the chart.

	Questions about hobbies	Answers
Notes from the video	What does Mark love?	
	What did he make into a car?	
	What changes did he make?	
	How long did it take?	
	How much did it cost?	
	What does he do with his car?	
My hobby	What is it?	
	How much does it cost?	
	How much time do you spend on it?	

C. EXTEND Think about one of your hobbies. Write your ideas in the chart above.

SAY WHAT YOU THINK

A. INVESTIGATE Go around the class. Ask the questions from the chart. When someone answers *yes*, write down his or her name. Try to write a different name for each question.

I ride a bicycle to class.

A: *Do you ride a bicycle to class?*
B: *Yes, I do.*

Question	Name
1. Do you belong to a club?	
2. Are you interested in books?	
3. Do you play tennis?	
4. Are you good at math?	
5. Are you on a sports team?	
6. Do you ride a bicycle to class?	
7. Do you get together with friends on Thursdays?	
8. Do you take any lessons?	

B. DISCUSS Share your answers with a group.

A: *Eric belongs to a soccer club.*
B: *Alex belongs to a soccer club, too.*

TIP FOR SUCCESS

Use the word *too* to add information. It has the same meaning as *also*.

SPEAKING

OBJECTIVE ▶   At the end of this unit, you are going to interview a classmate and introduce him or her to the class.

GRAMMAR *Part 1* **Simple present of** *be*

Use the verb *be* to identify and describe people and things.

TIP FOR SUCCESS

Statements with *be* are followed by nouns *(student)*, adjectives *(tired)*, or prepositional phrases *(from China)*.

Statements

subject	*be*	*(not)*	
I	**am / 'm**		a student.
You / We / They	**are / 're**	**(not)**	tired.
He / She / It	**is / 's**		from China.

- A contraction makes two words into one word. It has an apostrophe (').

  I am = I'm   You are = You're   They are = They're

  He is = He's   She is = She's   It is = It's

- You usually use contractions in speaking.

- There are two negative contractions for *are not*.

  are not = 're not / aren't

  They**'re not** happy.   They **aren't** tired.

- There are two negative contractions for *is not*.

  is not = 's not / isn't

  She**'s not** American.   He **isn't** from England.

Yes / No questions			Answers
be	subject		
Are	you / we / they	in class?	Yes, I **am**. / No, we**'re not**. / Yes, they **are**.
Is	he / she		No, she **isn't**. / Yes, he **is**.

Information questions				Answers
wh- word	*be*	subject		
What	**is**	she	interested in?	She**'s** interested in sports.
Where	**are**	they	from?	They**'re** from Morocco.
How old	**are**	you?		I**'m** 22 years old.

- You can give short answers or long answers:

  A: How old are you?

  B: 18. / I'm 18 years old.

A. APPLY Complete the sentences with the correct form of *be*.

1. Mauro _is_ an artist. He _isn't_ (not) from Colombia. He _is_ from Peru.

2. Rika and Emiko _are_ students. Rika _is_ in my English class. Emiko _is_ in my chemistry class. They _are_ from Japan.

3. Feride _are_ (not) American. She _is_ Turkish.

4. I _am_ (not) from England. I _am_ from Ireland.

5. We _are/n't_ (not) interested in sports. We _are_ interested in movies.

B. COMPOSE Put the words in the correct order. Then ask and answer the questions with a partner.

1. you / from / where / are _Where are you from?_

2. interested / hiking / you / in / are _Are you in interested?_

3. at / you / are / what / good _Good what are you at?_

4. years / 20 / old / you / are _Are you 20 old years?_

GRAMMAR *Part 2* Simple present of other verbs

Use the simple present with other verbs to describe habits, facts, and feelings.

Affirmative statements		
subject	verb	
I / You / We / They	**play**	soccer.
He / She	**plays**	tennis.

Negative statements			
subject	*do / does + not*	verb	
I / You / We / They	**do not / don't**	**play**	baseball.
He / She	**does not / doesn't**		

- Use *do not* with *I, we, you,* and *they*.
- Use *does not* with *he, she,* and *it*.

Yes / No questions			Answers
do / does	subject	verb	
Do	you / we / they	**like** tennis?	Yes, I **do**. / No, we **don't**. / Yes, they **do**.
Does	he / she		Yes, he **does**. / No, she **doesn't**.

Information questions				Answers
wh- word	*do / does*	subject		
What	**do**	you	play?	I play soccer.
Where	**does**	he	live?	He lives in Seoul.
When	**do**	they	study?	At 6:00.

- You can give short answers or long answers for these questions, too:

  A: Where do you live?

  B: In Tokyo. / I live in Tokyo.

iQ RESOURCES Go online to watch the Grammar Skill Video.
Resources > Video > Unit 1 > Grammar Skill Video

C. APPLY Complete the conversations with the verbs from the box. Use the correct form. You will use some verbs more than once. Then practice with a partner.

be	go	like	live	play	take

1. **Sara:** Mary, what _are_ you interested in?

   Mary: Well, I _go_ hiking on the weekends. And on Fridays, I _take_ French lessons.

2. **Emma:** _are_ your brother interested in sports?

   Mika: Yes, he _is_. He _plays_ soccer a lot.

3. **Anna:** _aren't_ your parents from China?

   Junko: No, they _are_. They _like_ from Japan, but they _are_ in the United States now.

4. **Joe:** _Are_ you good at Scrabble? I _play_ Scrabble a lot.

   Rob: No, I _'m not_ good at Scrabble. But my brothers _play_ Scrabble often.

Scrabble™

D. COMPOSE Put the words in the correct order. Then ask and answer the questions with a partner.

1. you / where / people / do / usually meet

   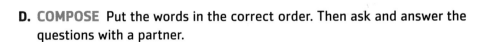
   You do People usually meet where

2. know / do / on your street / people / you

   Do You know People on your street

3. your / do / what / you do / with / friends

Your what do friends you with do

4. you / go / friends / where / with / your / do

your friends go where with you do ?

iQ PRACTICE Go online for more practice with the simple present of *be* and other verbs. *Practice > Unit 1 > Activities 7–8*

PRONUNCIATION Simple present third-person -s / -es

There are three ways to pronounce the final -*s* or -*es* of a simple present verb.

/ s /	/ z /	/ ɪz /
gets makes	listens plays	watches washes

A. IDENTIFY Listen to the sentences. Circle the sound that you hear at the end of the verb. Then practice the sentences with a partner.

1. He goes shopping on Saturdays. / s / **(/ z /)** / ɪz /
2. Khalid works downtown. **(/ s /)** / z / / ɪz /
3. Sam plays video games in the evening. / s / **(/ z /)** / ɪz /
4. Sun-Hee sometimes watches TV after work. / s / / z / **(/ ɪz /)**
5. Mary gets together with friends on Sundays. **(/ s /)** / z / / ɪz /
6. Mika lives in Los Angeles. / s / **(/ z /)** / ɪz /
7. David washes his car on Saturdays. / s / / z / **(/ ɪz /)**
8. Miteb belongs to a golf club. / s / **(/ z /)** / ɪz /

David washes his car.

B. CREATE Write five sentences about your friends. Use verbs from the box.

belongs	gets	goes	plays	takes	washes	watches

1. _____
2. _____
3. _____
4. _____
5. _____

C. CATEGORIZE Read your sentences from Activity B to a partner. For each of your partner's sentences, circle the sound you hear.

1. / s / / z / / ɪz /	3. / s / / z / / ɪz /	5. / s / / z / / ɪz /
2. / s / / z / / ɪz /	4. / s / / z / / ɪz /	

iQ PRACTICE Go online for more practice with simple present third-person verbs ending in -s and -es. *Practice ▸ Unit 1 ▸ Activity 9*

SPEAKING SKILL *Part 1* Keeping a conversation going

Adding information

Short answers to questions do not help conversations. Give extra information to keep your conversation going.

Answer is too short.	Answer is good.
A: Rome is my favorite city. What's yours? B: Shanghai.	A: Rome is my favorite city. What's yours? B: Shanghai. It has amazing buildings and delicious food!
A: I like cooking. How about you? B: I like cooking, too.	A: I like cooking. How about you? B: I like cooking, too. I often cook with friends on the weekends.

TIP FOR SUCCESS

Ask short questions like *How about you?* or *What's yours?* to get the other person's opinion or answer.

A. CREATE Write answers to the questions. Add extra information. Then ask and answer the questions with a partner.

1. A: What are your hobbies?

   B: _____

2. A: I like soccer. How about you?

   B: _____

3. A: What are you good at?

   B: *I am goo at cooking*

4. A: *Great Expectations* is my favorite book. What's yours?

   B: *my favori...*

5. A: Are you interested in history?

   B: _____

6. A: I'm interested in cooking. How about you?

   B: _____

Taking time to think

Sometimes you can't answer a question right away. Use these special expressions before you answer. They tell people, "I am thinking."

🔊 ⌐ Hmm.   Let's see.   Let me see.   Let me think.   Uh …   Well …

🔊 **B. APPLY** Listen to the conversation. Complete the sentences with the expressions you hear. Then practice the conversation with a partner.

Tom: Carlos, what's your favorite sport?

Carlos: _____, it's soccer. But I also like basketball. What's yours?
1

Tom: _____. It's probably volleyball. I play on the beach in the
2
summer.

Carlos: Where's your favorite beach?

Tom: _____. Miami has a really good beach.
3

Carlos: _____ , what's your favorite beach near here?
4

Tom: Ocean Beach is my favorite. It's beautiful! Do you know any beaches near here?

People surf at East Beach.

Carlos: _____. _____, I like East Beach. It has
5   6
really big waves. People surf there.

C. EXTEND Work with a partner. Practice the questions and answers in Activity A on page 16 again. Use special expressions like *Hmm* and *Let me think*.

> A: *What are your hobbies?*
> B: *Let me think. I like games. I play Scrabble a lot.*

iQ PRACTICE   Go online for more practice with keeping a conversation going.
Practice > Unit 1 > Activity 10

When you take notes, don't try to write down every word that you hear. Just write the important or meaningful words.

Read this sample from an interview.

> Michael: What's your name?
>
> Sung: My name is Sung-bo Shin. You can call me Sung.
>
> Michael: Where are you from?
>
> Sung: I'm from Seoul, South Korea.

> Michael: Do you have a job?
>
> Sung: Yes, I do. I'm a construction worker.
>
> Michael: What are you interested in?
>
> Sung: I like to swim and run. I also like to paint.

Look at the interviewer's notes. The interviewer only wrote the important words.

Sung-bo Shin (Sung)
Seoul, South Korea
construction worker
swimming, running, painting

UNIT ASSIGNMENT

OBJECTIVE ▶

Interview and introduce a classmate

In this assignment, you are going to interview a classmate and introduce him or her to the class. Think about the Unit Question, "What are you interested in?" Use the listening, the unit video, and your work in this unit. Look at the Self-Assessment checklist on page 20.

CONSIDER THE IDEAS

A. IDENTIFY What do you say in an introduction? Check (✓) the information.

☐ a greeting   ☐ favorite book

☐ telephone number   ☐ hobbies and interests

☐ country   ☐ name

☐ job

B. IDENTIFY Listen to this sample introduction. Then look at the list in Activity A. What information is in the introduction? Circle the ideas in Activity A.

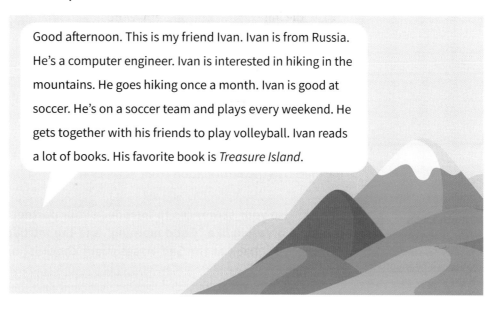

> Good afternoon. This is my friend Ivan. Ivan is from Russia. He's a computer engineer. Ivan is interested in hiking in the mountains. He goes hiking once a month. Ivan is good at soccer. He's on a soccer team and plays every weekend. He gets together with his friends to play volleyball. Ivan reads a lot of books. His favorite book is *Treasure Island*.

PREPARE AND SPEAK

A. FIND IDEAS Work with a partner. Follow these steps.

1. Add a question to the personal questionnaire below.

PERSONAL QUESTIONNAIRE

1. What's your name? _____

2. Where are you from? _____

3. What's your favorite book? _____

4. What's your favorite food? _____
   _____

5. What are your hobbies and interests? _____
   _____

6. What are you good at? _____
   _____

7. _____
   _____
   _____

2. Use the questions to interview your partner. Write your partner's answers in the questionnaire on page 19. Write only the important words.

3. When you answer the questions, give extra information (not just short answers). Use special expressions like *Hmm* and *Let me think*.

B. RESTATE Compare notes with your partner.

iQ PRACTICE Go online for more practice with writing important words. *Practice > Unit 1 > Activity 11*

C. ORGANIZE IDEAS Write three to five interesting sentences about your partner. Use the information from Activity A.

D. SPEAK Use your sentences to introduce your partner to the class. Include a greeting like "Good morning" and the introduction phrase "This is . . . ." Look at the Self-Assessment checklist below before you begin.

TIP FOR SUCCESS
In your presentation, speak clearly so your classmates can hear you. Look at the audience.

iQ PRACTICE Go online for your alternate Unit Assignment. *Practice > Unit 1 > Activity 12*

CHECK AND REFLECT

A. CHECK Think about the Unit Assignment as you complete the Self-Assessment checklist.

SELF-ASSESSMENT	Yes	No
My introduction was clear.	☐	☐
I used vocabulary from this unit.	☐	☐
I used the verb *be* and simple present statements correctly.	☐	☐
I included interesting information about my partner.	☐	☐
I took notes using only important words.	☐	☐

B. REFLECT Discuss these questions with a partner or group.

1. What is something new you learned in this unit?

2. Think about the Unit Question—What are you interested in? Is your answer different now than when you started this unit? If yes, how is it different? Why?

iQ PRACTICE Go to the online discussion board to discuss these questions. *Practice > Unit 1 > Activity 13*

TRACK YOUR SUCCESS

iQ PRACTICE Go online to check the words and phrases you have learned in this unit. *Practice > Unit 1 > Activity 14*

Check (✓) the skills you learned. If you need more work on a skill, refer to the page(s) in parentheses.

CRITICAL THINKING ☐ I can notice similarities between things. (pp. 6–7)

VOCABULARY ☐ I can understand collocations for hobbies and interests. (p. 8)

GRAMMAR ☐ I can use the simple present of *be* and other verbs. (pp. 12, 13–14)

PRONUNCIATION ☐ I can pronounce simple present third-person *-s / -es*. (p. 15)

SPEAKING ☐ I can keep a conversation going. (pp. 16, 17)

NOTE-TAKING ☐ I can write important words when taking notes. (p. 18)

OBJECTIVE ▶ ☐ I can use information and ideas to interview a classmate and introduce him or her to the class.

2 Education

What makes a good school?

A. Discuss these questions with your classmates.

1. How many students go to your school?

2. Does your school have any clubs or sports teams?

3. Look at the photo. Does your school have places like this one? What do students do there?

B. Listen to *The Q Classroom* online. Then answer these questions.

1. What did the students say? What does each student like in a school?

2. Who do you agree with? Which ideas are less important to you?

C. What do you want in a school? Complete the chart below. Check (✓) the correct column for each item.

	Very important	Important	Not important
sports	☐	☐	☐
clubs	☐	☐	☐
friends	☐	☐	☐
interesting classes	☐	☐	☐
sunny weather	☐	☐	☐
your own idea: _____	☐	☐	☐

iQ PRACTICE Go to the online discussion board to discuss the Unit Question with your classmates. *Practice > Unit 2 > Activity 1*

UNIT OBJECTIVE

Listen to a conversation. Use information and ideas to give a presentation about a perfect school.

Asking Questions about a University

You are going to listen to someone describe a university. Think about what makes a good school.

PREVIEW THE LISTENING

A. VOCABULARY Here are some words and phrases from the listening. Read the definitions. Then read the sentences. Which explanation is correct? Circle *a* or *b*.

---

campus *(noun)* 🔑 the buildings of a university or college and the land around them

community *(noun)* 🔑 OPAL all the people who live in a place

download *(verb)* 🔑 to get data from another computer, usually using the Internet

foreign language *(noun phrase)* 🔑 words that people from a different country say and write

online *(adjective, adverb)* 🔑 OPAL being connected to a computer or the Internet

professor *(noun)* 🔑 a teacher at a college or university

skill *(noun)* 🔑 OPAL the ability to do something well

special *(adjective)* 🔑 not ordinary or usual; different from what is normal

---

🔑 Oxford 3000™ words   **OPAL** Oxford Phrasal Academic Lexicon

1. My university has a big **campus**. It has more than 100 buildings.

   a. The classrooms are part of the campus.

   b. The students are part of the campus.

2. Sultan can't go **online** in his room. He goes to a cafe to check his email.

    a. Sultan can go on the Internet in his room.

    b. Sultan can't go on the Internet in his room.

3. Maryam has a great math **professor**. His classes are always interesting.

    a. A professor is a university student.

    b. A professor is a university teacher.

4. John gets good grades, so he is in **special** classes. His classes are difficult.

    a. John's classes are different or unusual.

    b. John's classes are normal or regular.

5. Ali can't **download** his email because he can't go online.

    a. Ali can't get his email.

    b. Ali has a lot of email.

6. Writing is an important **skill**. Huda writes every day. She wants to be a good writer.

    a. Playing tennis is also a skill.

    b. Watching television is also a skill.

7. David is from France. For David, Korean is a **foreign language**.

    a. French is also a foreign language for David.

    b. Spanish is also a foreign language for David.

8. A **community** is a group of people. They live or work in the same area.

    a. A bus stop is a kind of community.

    b. A town is a kind of community.

B. APPLY Complete the sentences with words and phrases from Activity A.

TIP FOR SUCCESS
The word *school* can refer to any educational institute. The words *college* and *university* often have the same meaning: a place of higher education with degree programs.

1. At my school, all the students study a _____. I'm in a Japanese class.

2. Fahad's university has a really small _____. You can walk across it in ten minutes.

3. A class is a kind of _____. The teachers and students work together.

4. I have to talk to my biology _____. I have a question about the test.

5. My brother _____ a lot of books from the Internet. He reads them on his phone or on his tablet.

6. Reading is an important _____. Good students read well.

iQ PRACTICE Go online for more practice with the vocabulary.
Practice > Unit 2 > Activities 2–3

C. PREVIEW You are going to listen to two people talk about Al Jaser Online University. What do you think you can do at an online university? Check (✓) your answers.

☐ be part of a community   ☐ play sports

☐ live in a dormitory   ☐ watch lectures

☐ get books from a library   ☐ eat in a dining hall

☐ meet other students   ☐ take classes at any time

D. IDENTIFY Read the questions. Circle *Yes* or *No*.

1. Does your school have a library?	Yes	No
2. Does it have a dormitory?	Yes	No
3. Does it have Internet access?	Yes	No

E. CREATE What are some other things at your school?

_____

_____

WORK WITH THE LISTENING

🔊 **A. CATEGORIZE** Read the sentences. Listen to the conversation. Write *T* (true) or *F* (false). Then correct the false statements.

iQ RESOURCES Go online to download extra vocabulary support.
Resources > Extra Vocabulary > Unit 2

_____ 1. The classes are online.

_____

_____ 2. The university has a campus.

_____

_____ 3. Students can practice foreign languages with other students.

_____

_____ 4. The school has about 2,000 students.

_____

_____ 5. All the students live in the Middle East.

_____

_____ 6. The professors live all over the world.

_____

B. IDENTIFY Read the questions. Then circle the correct answer.

1. Who is Sarah?

    a. an employee at Al Jaser Online University

    b. a student at Al Jaser Online University

    c. a new student

2. Why does Layla call?

    a. She is a new student.

    b. She wants information about the school.

    c. She wants a job.

3. What is special about this university?

    a. Students can only study a few subjects.

    b. Students come from many different countries.

    c. It's small, so you can talk to your professors every day.

iQ PRACTICE Go online for additional listening and comprehension.
Practice > Unit 2 > Activity 4

LISTENING SKILL Listening for examples

People give examples with *like*. *Like* comes in the middle of a sentence.

⌐ I study in different places, **like** the library or my dormitory.

People also give examples with *for example*. *For example* can come at the beginning of a sentence.

⌐ Watson University has many interesting classes. **For example**, I have classes in
└ French and history.

IDENTIFY Listen again to the conversation about Al Jaser Online University.
Listen for examples with *for example* or *like*. Circle the correct answer.

1. What can you talk about in a chat room at Al Jaser Online University?

    a. science   c. sports

    b. math   d. history

2. What else can you do in a chat room at Al Jaser?

    a. talk with professors   c. practice French

    b. talk about tests   d. watch lectures

3. At Al Jaser Online University, you can join a club. What examples does Sarah give?

    a. book club and math club   c. science club and math club

    b. French club and science club   d. science club and book club

4. Where do some of the professors live?

    a. Japan and England   c. England, Saudi Arabia, and France

    b. France and Canada   d. Saudi Arabia, France, and Japan

5. What kinds of classes can students take at Al Jaser?

    a. history, math, and science

    b. foreign languages, history, and sports

    c. math, computers, and science

    d. history, art, and music

iQ PRACTICE Go online for more practice with listening for examples.
Practice > Unit 2 > Activity 5

NOTE-TAKING SKILL Taking notes on examples

It is good to write down examples. Writing them in a chart helps you remember them. Listen to two students talk about a college. Then look at the chart below. It shows examples of things the students talk about.

Mosa's college		
Classes	**Sports teams**	**Clubs**
history	tennis	book
math	soccer	hiking
	baseball	

CATEGORIZE Listen again to part of the conversation about Al Jaser Online University. Work with a partner to complete the chart with examples.

Al Jaser Online University		
Foreign language chat rooms	Things you can download at the library	Where students are from
French		

iQ PRACTICE Go online for more practice with taking notes on examples.
Practice ⟩ Unit 2 ⟩ Activity 6

BUILDING VOCABULARY Using the dictionary: antonyms

Antonyms are words with opposite meanings. For example, *good* and *bad* are antonyms. Most forms of words—nouns, verbs, adjectives, adverbs, and prepositions—can have antonyms.

The dictionary often gives antonyms in the definition of a word. In the example below, notice the antonyms of *hard*.

> **hard¹** /hɑrd/ *adjective* (hard·er, hard·est)
> **1** not soft: *These apples are very hard.* ◆ *I couldn't sleep because the bed was too hard.* ⊃ ANTONYM **soft**
> **2** difficult to do or understand: *The exam was very hard.* ◆ *hard work* ⊃ ANTONYM **easy**
> **3** full of problems: *He's had a hard life.* ⊃ ANTONYM **easy**
> **4** not kind or gentle: *She is very hard on her children.* ⊃ ANTONYM **soft**

All dictionary entries adapted from the *Oxford Basic American Dictionary for learners of English* © Oxford University Press 2011.

A. APPLY Write an antonym for each word. Use the words in the box. Use your dictionary to help you.

above	cheap	easy	strength
badly	complicated	negative	succeed

1. hard _____

2. fail _____

3. below _____

4. weakness _____

5. positive _____

6. simple _____

7. expensive __ _____

8. well _____

B. IDENTIFY Read the sentences. Circle the correct answer.

1. Min-seo doesn't like her school. The classrooms are always (clean / dirty).

2. In my history class, we have many discussions and presentations. I like it a lot. It's very (interesting / boring).

3. One (strength / weakness) of my school is the library. It's very small, and it doesn't have a lot of books.

4. The school is in a (safe / dangerous) part of town. Don't go out late at night.

5. My school costs a lot of money. It's very (cheap / expensive).

6. In a good school, all the students (fail / succeed).

7. Sarah lives (on / off) campus. Her dormitory is near the library.

8. My math class is really (easy / hard). I know all the answers.

C. COMPOSE Choose three adjectives. Write a sentence for each adjective and its antonym.

My chemistry class is <u>hard</u>.   Math is <u>easy</u> for me.

_____

_____

_____

_____

_____

_____

dormitory room

iQ PRACTICE   Go online for more practice with using the dictionary.
Practice > Unit 2 > Activity 7

WORK WITH THE VIDEO

A. PREVIEW What is hard about going to a new school?

VIDEO VOCABULARY

originally (adv.) in the beginning

actually (adv.) really; in fact

basically (adv.) in the most important ways

hand in hand (phr.) closely connected

homemade (adj.) made at home, not bought at a store

iQ RESOURCES Go online to watch the video about school in Japan.
Resources > Video > Unit 2 > Unit Video

B. CATEGORIZE Watch the video two or three times. Take notes in the first part of the chart.

	Things Sophie liked about her Japanese high school	My opinion about those things
Notes from the video		
My ideas		

C. EXTEND Do you like the same things Sophie liked? Write *Agree* or *Disagree* in the chart above. What are some ways the Japanese school is different from your school? Write your ideas in the chart above.

SAY WHAT YOU THINK

SYNTHESIZE Think about the listening and the unit video as you discuss the questions.

1. Which kind of school do you like better? Why?

2. What are some good things about each school?

3. How important is it to meet with other students and teachers in person? Why?

SPEAKING

OBJECTIVE ▶

At the end of this unit, you are going to give a group presentation about a perfect school.

GRAMMAR Adjectives; Adverbs + adjectives

Adjectives

1. Adjectives describe nouns (people, places, things, or ideas).

   • An adjective can come after the verb *be*. It describes the subject.

subject	*be*	adjective
The school	is	**large.**
The students	are	**smart.**

   • An adjective can come before a noun. It describes the noun.

	adjective	noun
It's a	**safe**	**school.**
I have	**good**	**classes.**

2. There are no singular or plural adjectives.

   ✓ Correct: They are **interesting classes**.
   ✗ Incorrect: They are interestings classes.

3. Do not use an article (*the*, *a*, or *an*) before an adjective with no noun.

   ✓ Correct: The class is **interesting**.
   ✗ Incorrect: The class is an interesting.

Adverbs + adjectives

1. Adverbs make adjectives stronger.

   It's a **pretty** interesting class.   It's a **very** safe school.
   That school is **really** safe!   This classroom is **extremely** noisy!

   • Use *pretty* in speaking and informal writing. Don't use it in papers for your classes.

2. You can use *pretty*, *really*, *very*, and *extremely* before:

   an adjective alone: That school is **really excellent**.
   an adjective + a noun: It's a **very active class**.

iQ RESOURCES Go online to watch the Grammar Skill Video.
Resources ❯ Video ❯ Unit 2 ❯ Grammar Skill Video

A. IDENTIFY Read the paragraph. Find the ten adjective and adverb errors and correct them.

> new university
> Well, I am now at my ~~university new~~. It's in a large very city. It's pretty
> different from our small town. It's an extremely noisy, but I love it. There
> are excellents museums and parks. I live in an apartment expensive in the
> city. The building is beautiful really, but it's pretty old. My school is great,
> but my classes are big extremely. Some of my classes have 200 people
> in them! But my professors are a very good, and my classes are really
> interesting. We have a science laboratory great. I study biology there. Also,
> the people here are friendly very, but I miss my old friends.

B. COMPOSE Complete the conversation with adjectives or adverbs +
adjectives. Use your own ideas. Then practice with a partner.

A: Do you like this school?

B: Yes, I do. I think that it's a _____ _____ school.
What do you think?

A: I like it, too. The teachers are _____, and the classes are

_____ .

B: What do you think of the library?

A: I think that it's _____ _____ . What do you think
of the campus?

B: I think that it's _____ _____ .

a university library

iQ PRACTICE Go online for more practice with adjectives and adverbs + adjectives. *Practice › Unit 2 › Activity 8*

iQ PRACTICE Go online for the Grammar Expansion: adverbs of degree and the adverb *too*. *Practice › Unit 2 › Activity 9*

PRONUNCIATION Sentence stress

When you speak, you **stress** certain **important words**. This means you say them a little more loudly.

Important words—like nouns, adjectives, and adverbs—give the information in the sentences.

You do not usually stress words like pronouns, prepositions, *a / an / the*, the verb *be*, or the verb *do*.

🔊
> There are **two sports fields**.
> The **museum** is **not interesting**.
> We **go** to **school** in a **really dangerous neighborhood**.
> Do you **have** a **class today**?

🔊 **A. IDENTIFY** <u>Underline</u> the stressed words. Listen and check your answers. Then practice the sentences with a partner.

1. Does the school have a fencing team?

2. I have two classes in the morning.

3. We want a safe and clean school.

4. The college is in a dangerous city.

5. The coffee shops have free Internet access.

6. What is a good school?

7. Our sports field is pretty big.

8. My school is really great!

B. COMPOSE Write five sentences about your school. Use adjectives and the adverbs *pretty*, *really*, *very*, and *extremely*.

C. IDENTIFY Work with a partner. Read each other's sentences. Underline the stressed words. Then practice the sentences.

fencing

The <u>campus</u> is <u>extremely</u> <u>large</u>.

iQ PRACTICE Go online for more practice with sentence stress. *Practice › Unit 2 › Activity 10*

An **opinion** is something that a person thinks or feels. Use the phrases
I think that . . . and *In my opinion, . . .* to give an opinion.

> **I think that** students need computers.
> **In my opinion,** small classes are important.

You can answer opinions with *I agree* or *I disagree* followed by your opinion.

> A: **I think that** our school is great.
> B: **I agree.** I think that the classes are interesting.
> C: **I disagree.** In my opinion, the classes are too big.

A. IDENTIFY Listen and complete the conversations. Use expressions from the box above. Compare your answers with a partner.

1. A: _____ a good school gives a lot of tests.
   Then students study every day.

   B: _____. Class discussions make students study.

2. A: _____ sports are really important. Students need
   healthy bodies.

   B: _____. Exercise is very important.

3. A: _____ the food in our dining hall isn't very good. I don't
   like it!

   B: _____. _____ it tastes terrible. I usually cook
   my own food.

4. A: Our school isn't in a good neighborhood. _____ it's very
   dangerous. I hear police sirens all the time.

   B: _____. You hear sirens because the police station is on the
   same street! _____ the school is very safe.

ACADEMIC LANGUAGE
The corpus shows
that *I think that* is a
common phrase in
academic speaking.

_____ OPAL
Oxford Phrasal Academic Lexicon

TIP FOR SUCCESS
When you write *In my
opinion*, use a comma
after it. Don't use a
comma after *I think that*.

B. CREATE Write answers to the questions. Start your answers with *I think that* or *In my opinion*. Then ask and answer the questions with a partner.

1. What is the perfect number of students in a foreign language class?

2. In your opinion, what makes a class interesting? Give two ideas.

3. Do you think it's better to work alone or with a group? Why?

iQ PRACTICE Go online for more practice with giving your opinion.
Practice ⟩ Unit 2 ⟩ Activity 11

CRITICAL THINKING STRATEGY

Giving reasons for opinions

It is not enough to say your opinion. Explain *why* you think so. Give reasons for your opinion to make it stronger. Ask yourself *why*.

Opinion	Reason (*Why?*)
I think that it's important to have good friends at school.	Good friends can support me and help me study.
It's not important to have good friends at school.	It's more difficult to study with my friends because we chat a lot.

iQ PRACTICE   **Go online to watch the Critical Thinking Video and check your comprehension.** *Practice > Unit 2 > Activity 12*

C. EVALUATE Give your opinion of the following statements. Circle *Yes* or *No*. Think about the reasons for your opinion.

WHAT MAKES A GOOD SCHOOL AND A GOOD EDUCATIONAL EXPERIENCE?

1.	Yes	No	It's important to learn a foreign language in school.
2.	Yes	No	It's important to have good friends at school.
3.	Yes	No	Every school needs a lot of clubs and teams.
4.	Yes	No	A good school has computers for students to use.
5.	Yes	No	Every campus needs a library and a sports field.
6.	Yes	No	Good schools have small classes.
7.	Yes	No	A good school has a large campus.
8.	Yes	No	A good school is a community.
9.	Yes	No	A good school has new buildings.
10.	Yes	No	Good schools are always in big cities.
11.	Yes	No	In good schools, students can talk to teachers outside of class.
12.	Yes	No	In a good class, students can ask the teacher questions.

D. DISCUSS Discuss your answers with a partner. Give reasons for your opinions. Use *I think that* and *In my opinion* to give your opinions.

UNIT ASSIGNMENT
OBJECTIVE ▶

Plan a perfect school

In this assignment, you are going to plan a perfect school. This can be a high school, university, or other kind of school. Then you are going to present your plan to the class. Think about the Unit Question, "What makes a good school?" Use the listening, the unit video, and your work in this unit. Look at the Self-Assessment checklist on page 38.

CONSIDER THE IDEAS

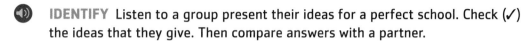

IDENTIFY Listen to a group present their ideas for a perfect school. Check (✓) the ideas that they give. Then compare answers with a partner.

- ☐ 1. The perfect school is large.
- ☐ 2. The classes are very small.
- ☐ 3. The school has a lot of clubs, like a book club and a soccer club.
- ☐ 4. There is a big gym.
- ☐ 5. Students get free computers.
- ☐ 6. The school is in a big city.
- ☐ 7. Apartments in town are cheap and beautiful.
- ☐ 8. Food on campus is cheap.

PREPARE AND SPEAK

TIP FOR SUCCESS

Examples can make your opinion strong and clear: *I think that a good school needs a sports field, like a soccer field. Students need exercise. It makes them healthy.*

A. FIND IDEAS Work with a group. Write answers for these questions. Use *I think that* and *In my opinion* to share your ideas. Give a reason for each opinion.

1. Is your perfect school big or small? How many students are in a class?

2. What does the school have? For example, does it have a swimming pool? Does it have computers?

3. Is your school in a big city or a small town? What can students do there?

4. What is special about your school? How is it different from other schools?

B. ORGANIZE IDEAS Work with your group. Prepare your presentation.

1. Each group member chooses at least one question from Activity A.

2. Write your part of the presentation. Include at least one example or reason for your idea.

3. First speaker: Use these sentences as your introduction.

   Good (morning / afternoon / evening). Today we are presenting our plan for the perfect school.

4. Last speaker: Use these sentences as your conclusion.

   That's the end of our presentation. Thank you. Do you have any questions?

C. SPEAK Present your ideas to your class. Look at the Self-Assessment checklist below before you begin.

iQ PRACTICE Go online for your alternate Unit Assignment.
Practice > Unit 2 > Activity 13

CHECK AND REFLECT

A. CHECK Think about the Unit Assignment as you complete the Self-Assessment checklist.

SELF-ASSESSMENT	Yes	No
I gave my opinion clearly.	☐	☐
I gave a reason for my opinion.	☐	☐
I used vocabulary from this unit.	☐	☐
I used adjectives and adverbs + adjectives correctly.	☐	☐
I stressed words in sentences correctly.	☐	☐

B. REFLECT Discuss these questions with a partner or group.

1. What is something new you learned in this unit?

2. Think about the Unit Question—What makes a good school? Is your answer different now than when you started this unit? If yes, how is it different? Why?

iQ PRACTICE Go to the online discussion board to discuss these questions.
Practice > Unit 2 > Activity 14

TRACK YOUR SUCCESS

iQ PRACTICE Go online to check the words and phrases you have learned in this unit. *Practice > Unit 2 > Activity 15*

Check (✓) the skills you learned. If you need more work on a skill, refer to the page(s) in parentheses.

LISTENING	☐ I can identify examples. (p. 27)
NOTE-TAKING	☐ I can take notes on examples. (p. 28)
VOCABULARY	☐ I can use the dictionary to understand antonyms. (p. 29)
GRAMMAR	☐ I can use adjectives and adverbs + adjectives. (p. 32)
PRONUNCIATION	☐ I can stress important words. (p. 34)
SPEAKING	☐ I can give my opinion. (p. 35)
CRITICAL THINKING	☐ I can give reasons for my opinion. (p. 36)

OBJECTIVE ▶ ☐ I can use information and ideas to present a plan about a perfect school.

3 Cultural Studies

? UNIT QUESTION

How do you choose your food?

A. Discuss these questions with your classmates.

1. Circle the adjectives that describe food. Compare with a partner.

active	delicious	healthy	sour
close	difficult	important	spicy
dangerous	fresh	salty	sweet

2. What kind of food do you like to eat? Where do you get it?

3. Look at the photo. Where do you think these people get their food?

 **B. Listen to *The Q Classroom* online. Then answer these questions.**

1. What did the students say about the foods they like?

2. Which student likes spicy food? Who doesn't eat much sugar? Who likes convenience?

3. Which student is similar to you in food tastes? For example, do you like spicy food? Why or why not?

iQ PRACTICE Go to the online discussion board to discuss the Unit Question with your classmates. *Practice > Unit 3 > Activity 1*

UNIT OBJECTIVE

Listen to a podcast. Use information and ideas to design a survey and interview a classmate.

Lifestyles and Food Choices

OBJECTIVE ▶

You are going to listen to a podcast about healthy food choices. Think about what makes food healthy.

PREVIEW THE LISTENING

A. VOCABULARY Here are some words from the listening. Read the definitions. Then complete the sentences below.

ACADEMIC LANGUAGE

Avoid is one of the most common words used in academic speaking and writing.

⎯⎯⎯⎯⎯ OPAL
Oxford Phrasal Academic Lexicon

avoid *(verb)* 🔑 OPAL to try not to do something; to stay away from something

flavor *(noun)* 🔑 the taste of food, like salty or sweet

ingredient *(noun)* 🔑 one of the things that are used to make food

memory *(noun)* 🔑 the ability to remember things

nutritious *(adjective)* good for you

organic *(adjective)* natural; organic food has only natural ingredients

vegetarian *(noun)* a person who does not eat meat

🔑 Oxford 3000™ words   **OPAL** Oxford Phrasal Academic Lexicon

1. I put tomato sauce, garlic, cheese, and onions in my pasta. It has a lot of
   _____.

2. Fruits are _____. For example, oranges have vitamin C.

3. Amir has a good _____ for faces. He remembers everyone he sees.

4. Amanda and Matt _____ food with a lot of fat. For example, they don't eat French fries or cheeseburgers.

5. Lemons are sour, but oranges have a sweet _____.

6. Sam doesn't eat chicken or beef. He's a _____.

7. John buys his food at a health-food store. He eats only _____ food.

TIP FOR SUCCESS

Artificial means not natural or real. Some food has artificial ingredients. These are made by people.

B. Answer the questions. Then compare with a partner.

1. What is an example of a food with a strong flavor? _____

2. Are you a vegetarian or do you eat meat? _____

3. How often do you eat organic food? _____

4. Do you avoid food with artificial ingredients? _____
   Why or why not? _____

5. Name three foods that are very nutritious. _____
   _____

iQ PRACTICE   Go online for more practice with the vocabulary.
Practice > Unit 3 > Activities 2 3

C. PREVIEW You are going to listen to a podcast about healthy food choices. Look at the pictures. Check (✓) the kinds of food you eat. How healthy are they? Write 1 (not healthy), 2 (a little healthy), or 3 (very healthy).

☐ meat ____   ☐ vegetables ____   ☐ fruit ____

☐ dessert ____   ☐ dairy ____   ☐ grains ____

Speakers use reasons to explain their actions. In conversations, speakers often use *why* to ask for reasons. They use *because* to give reasons.

A: **Why** do you eat sugar-free food?

B: **Because** sugar is bad for your teeth.

A: **Why** don't you eat fast food?

B: **Because** it has artificial ingredients in it.

Listen for these two key words—*why* and *because*—to understand reasons.

A. IDENTIFY Read the sentences. Then listen to the conversations. Circle the correct answer.

1. Why does John buy only organic apples?

   a. Because they are cheap.

   b. Because they're good for him.

   c. Because he likes the flavor.

   d. Because they're sweet.

2. Why does Amanda avoid fattening foods?

   a. Because she doesn't like them.

   b. Because she wants to lose weight.

   c. Because they're bad for her health.

   d. Because she's allergic.

3. Why does James want to go out for dinner?

   a. Because his friend is a terrible cook.

   b. Because he is a terrible cook.

   c. Because it's cheap.

   d. Because he doesn't have any food at home.

4. Kay's Kitchen is Anna's favorite restaurant. Why?

   a. Because it's near her house.

   b. Because their food is delicious.

   c. Because their food is cheap.

   d. Because it's organic.

B. EXPLAIN Are you similar to John, Amanda, James, or Anna? Tell your classmates.

I think I'm similar to John. We both like organic food.

fattening foods

iQ PRACTICE Go online for more practice with listening for reasons.
Practice > Unit 3 > Activity 4

WORK WITH THE LISTENING

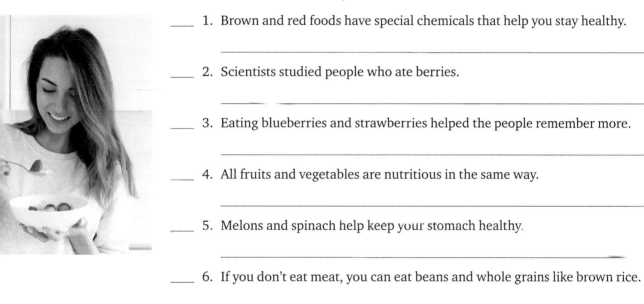

A. **CATEGORIZE** Listen to the podcast about berries. Read the statements. Write *T* (true) or *F* (false). Then correct the false statements.

iQ RESOURCES Go online to download extra vocabulary support.
Resources > Extra Vocabulary > Unit 3

____ 1. Brown and red foods have special chemicals that help you stay healthy.

_____

____ 2. Scientists studied people who ate berries.

_____

____ 3. Eating blueberries and strawberries helped the people remember more.

_____

____ 4. All fruits and vegetables are nutritious in the same way.

_____

____ 5. Melons and spinach help keep your stomach healthy.

_____

____ 6. If you don't eat meat, you can eat beans and whole grains like brown rice.

_____

B. **APPLY** Listen again. Circle the correct answer.

1. How many people did the researchers study?

   a. 16,000

   b. 1,600

   c. 160

2. What are other red or blue foods Anya talks about?

   a. beans, tomatoes, and beets

   b. melons, tomatoes, and meat

   c. cherries, peppers, and beans

3. What other color foods are healthy?

   a. green and purple

   b. white and pink

   c. orange and green

4. Why should you eat organic fruits and vegetables?

   a. They taste better.

   b. They are more nutritious.

   c. They are better for the environment.

5. What does Anya suggest you put on a sandwich?

   a. spinach

   b. tomatoes

   c. cheese

 CRITICAL THINKING STRATEGY

Recognizing cause and effect

Speakers often describe cause and effect relationships. A **cause** is like a reason. It can make something happen—which is the **effect**. An effect is an outcome or result.

The words and phrases *because*, *because of*, and *since* can introduce a cause. The word *so* introduces an effect. Verbs like *help*, *cause*, and *give* can introduce effects, too.

Other cause-effect relationships are not stated as directly. Think about the relationship between the two things. The cause can come first or second in the sentence.

Cause	Effect
Because I love animals,	I don't eat meat.
I love animals,	**so** I don't eat meat.
Dairy products	**help** build strong bones.

Sometimes the effect of one action is also the cause of another.

   cause   →   effect and cause   →   effect

   Because *I love animals, I don't eat meat, **so** I eat whole grains, beans, and nuts instead.*

iQ PRACTICE Go online to watch the Critical Thinking Video and check your comprehension. *Practice > Unit 3 > Activity 5*

C. **ANALYZE** Listen again. Match the cause with its effect.

Cause	Effect
1. special chemicals that give food red and blue color ____	a. get the same health benefits
2. eating more berries ____	b. decision to eat berries every day
3. the results of the research ____	c. better memories
4. orange and green foods ____	d. help keep us healthy, and keep our brains in good shape
5. being a vegetarian ____	e. keep your heart healthy
6. using fruits and vegetables as ingredients ____	f. eat a lot of fruits and vegetables

D. **RESTATE** Answer the questions.

1. Why should we eat berries? _____

2. What happened in the study? _____

_____

3. What foods are part of a healthy diet according to Anya?

_____

iQ PRACTICE Go online to listen to *Breakfast in Different Countries* and check your comprehension. *Practice > Unit 3 > Activity 6*

A **prefix** comes at the beginning of a word. It changes the meaning of the word. A **suffix** comes at the end of a word. It often changes the part of speech. Learners' dictionaries usually give definitions for prefixes and suffixes. Other dictionaries often list them at the back.

The prefixes *non-* and *un-* mean "not." The suffix *-free* means "without," and it changes a noun (*sugar*) into an adjective (*sugar-free*). Look at the definitions.

Prefix
non- not: **non**fiction (= *writing that is about real people, events*) ◆ *a **non**stop flight*

Suffix
-free (in adjectives) not containing the (usually bad) thing mentioned: *sugar-**free** cola* ◆ *fat-**free** yogurt* ◆ *a smoke-**free** environment* ◆ *a tax-**free** savings account*

Prefix
un- not; the opposite of: **un**happy ◆ **un**true (= *not true*) ◆ **un**lock ◆ **un**dress (= *to take clothes off*)

All dictionary entries adapted from the *Oxford Basic American Dictionary for learners of English* © Oxford University Press 2011.

A. APPLY Complete each sentence with a word from the box.

nondairy	salt-free	unfriendly	unsafe
nonfat	sugar-free	unhealthy	unusual

I'm allergic to food with milk.

OIL SHORTENING (PARTIALLY
D SOYBEAN OIL, PROPYLENE
AND DIESTERS OF FATS, MC
ERIDES). CONTAINS 2% OR
NG (SODIUM BICARBONATE
M PHOSPHATE), DEXTROSE, N
TARCH, SALT, CELLULOSE GU
RIN, ARTIFICIAL FLAVORS, C
ELLOW 5 LAKE, RED 40 LAK

artificial ingredients

☐ 1. I worry about foods with a lot of fat. I drink only _____ milk.

☐ 2. I eat a lot of junk food, like chips, cookies, and cake. I never exercise. I'm often sick. I'm very _____.

☐ 3. She doesn't talk to anyone. She's very _____.

☐ 4. I'm allergic to food with milk, cheese, or butter. I eat only _____ food.

☐ 5. I don't eat food with a lot of salt in it. Salt is bad for my health. I try to eat _____ food.

☐ 6. I only eat organic food. I think food with artificial ingredients is _____.

☐ 7. I avoid food and drinks with sugar. I try to have only _____ food and drinks.

☐ 8. I like to try _____ foods. I don't like to eat the same kind of food every day.

B. **IDENTIFY** Check (✓) the items in Activity A that are true for you. Then compare your answers with a partner.

C. **EXTEND** Find two more prefixes or suffixes in your dictionary. Write three sentences with those words that have those prefixes or suffixes.

iQ PRACTICE Go online for more practice with prefixes and suffixes.
Practice > Unit 3 > Activity 7

PRONUNCIATION Stressed syllables

In words with two or more syllables, you usually **stress one syllable**. You say the syllable with more energy. In these words, the bold syllables are stressed.

 or • **gan** • ic   veg • e • **tar** • i • an   un • **friend** • ly

 A. **IDENTIFY** Listen to the words. Circle the stressed syllables. Then practice with a partner.

1. de • li • cious
2. al • ler • gic
3. un • health • y
4. ed • u • ca • tion
5. in • gre • di • ent

6. sug • ar • free
7. gar • den
8. din • ner
9. non • dai • ry
10. com • mu • ni • ty

 B. **APPLY** Listen to the sentences. Circle the stressed syllables in words with two or more syllables.

TIP FOR SUCCESS
We usually don't stress words like pronouns, prepositions, and articles. See the Pronunciation box on page 34 for more information.

1. In my opinion, artificial ingredients are unsafe.
2. He doesn't eat chicken or beef.
3. He wants to lose weight, so he's on a diet.
4. This soup has an unusual flavor.
5. Are these cookies sugar-free?
6. She grows organic tomatoes in her garden.

C. **EXTEND** Listen again. Underline the stressed words in the sentences.

iQ PRACTICE Go online for more practice with stressed syllables.
Practice > Unit 3 > Activity 8

WORK WITH THE VIDEO

A. PREVIEW Do you like to buy food at farmers' markets? Why? Why not?

VIDEO VOCABULARY

fresh (adj.) made or picked recently

local (adj.) from a place near you

crisp (adj.) firm and fresh

juicy (adj.) full of juice

iQ RESOURCES Go online to watch the video about shopping at a farmers' market. *Resources > Video > Unit 3 > Unit Video*

B. CATEGORIZE Watch the video two or three times. Take notes in the first part of the chart.

	Things Jean wants to buy	Things she doesn't need to buy
Notes from the video		
My ideas		

C. EXTEND What are other things you can buy at a farmers' market? What are things you can't usually buy at a farmers' market? Write your ideas in the chart above.

SAY WHAT YOU THINK

A. COMPOSE Think about the listening and the unit video. Answer these questions.

Food Survey

1. Do you eat meat? Why or why not?

   _____

   _____

2. Do you eat fast food? Why or why not?

   _____

3. Do you eat organic food? Why or why not?

   _____

4. Do you eat food with artificial ingredients? Why or why not?

   _____

5. What kinds of food do you usually eat? Why do you choose them?

   _____

   _____

6. What's your favorite food? Why?

   _____

7. What kinds of food do you avoid? Why?

   _____

   _____

8. What do you usually eat for breakfast?

   _____

TIP FOR SUCCESS
You can use *Why **don't** you . . . ?* or *Why **doesn't** he / she . . . ?* to ask why someone *doesn't* do something.

B. DISCUSS Discuss your answers with a partner.

A: *Do you eat meat?*

B: *Yes, I do.*

A: *Why?*

B: *Because it's delicious and I like the flavor.*

SPEAKING

OBJECTIVE ▶

At the end of this unit, you are going to design a survey about food and interview a classmate.

GRAMMAR Verbs + gerunds or infinitives

1. Gerunds and infinitives are usually words for activities.

   • A gerund is a **base verb** + **-ing**: *eating, cooking, baking.*

   • An infinitive is **to** + a **base verb**: *to eat, to cook, to bake.*

2. **Verbs + gerunds** You can use gerunds after these verbs.

subject	verb	gerund
We	enjoy	cooking.
I	avoid	buying fast food.

3. **Verbs + infinitives** You can use infinitives after these verbs.

subject	verb	infinitive
He	tries	to eat only organic food.
We	need	to make dinner.
They	want	to eat only healthy food.

4. **Verbs + gerunds *or* infinitives** You can use gerunds or infinitives after these verbs.

subject	verb	gerund or infinitive
He	likes	to eat at home. eating at home.
We	hate	to shop at Bob's Market. shopping at Bob's Market.
They	love	to go out to dinner. going out to dinner.
I	can't stand	to cook. cooking.

iQ RESOURCES   Go online to watch the Grammar Skill Video.
Resources › Video › Unit 3 › Grammar Skill Video

A. IDENTIFY **Listen to the sentences. What do you hear? Circle the gerund or infinitive.**

1. to cook / cooking
2. to eat / eating
3. to shop / shopping
4. to buy / buying
5. to eat / eating

6. to avoid / avoiding
7. to cook / cooking
8. to eat / eating
9. to eat / eating
10. to go / going

B. APPLY **Complete the conversation with the correct infinitive or gerund forms. In some sentences, both a gerund and an infinitive are correct.**

Mary: Sun-Hee, I have to make dinner for my husband's parents on Friday night. I'm so nervous. Can you help me?

Sun-Hee: Sure, I love _____ (cook). What kinds of food do they like
1
_____ (eat)?
2

Mary: Well, my mother-in-law enjoys _____ (try) new things,
3
but my father-in-law avoids _____ (eat) a lot of different things.
4
For example, he's allergic to dairy foods, and he tries _____ (avoid) foods
5
with a lot of salt

Sun-Hee: What do they like?

Mary: Um, they like chicken and fish. And they like vegetables.

Sun-Hee: All right. I have a great recipe for roast chicken and vegetables. It's spicy, but it's not very salty.

Mary: That sounds perfect! Thanks so much. I try _____ (cook), but I'm
6
not very good in the kitchen.

Sun-Hee: No problem. What time do you want _____ (start)?
7

Mary: How about 3:00?

Sun-Hee: Great! I'll see you then!

spicy

C. COMPOSE Complete the sentences with information about food. Use a verb + infinitive or gerund from the box in each sentence. Share your ideas with a partner.

avoid	buy	drink	feel	go	have	make
bake	cook	eat	find	grow	listen	tell

1. I want _to grow a garden at home_____.

2. I need _____.

3. I try _____   _____.

4. I like _____.

5. I love _____.

6. I hate _____.

iQ PRACTICE   Go online for more practice with verbs + gerunds or infinitives. *Practice > Unit 3 > Activities 9–10*

UNIT ASSIGNMENT
OBJECTIVE ▶

Design a survey and interview a classmate

In this assignment, you are going to design a survey and interview a classmate about his or her food choices. Think about the Unit Question, "How do you choose your food?" Use the listening, the unit video, and your work in this unit. Look at the Self-Assessment checklist on page 56.

CONSIDER THE IDEAS

IDENTIFY Listen to the interview. Match the questions with the student's answers.

1. What's your favorite food? _____   a. Because I'm allergic to them.

2. Do you think organic food is good for you? _____   b. Nonfat yogurt with fruit and nuts.

3. Why do you avoid strawberries? _____   c. I don't know.

4. What do you usually eat for breakfast? _____   d. I think it's healthy.

5. Why do you have that? _____   e. Pizza.

PREPARE AND SPEAK

A. FIND IDEAS Work with a partner. Write ten interview questions.

- Write questions about food likes, dislikes, choices, and opinions.

- Include questions with gerunds and infinitives.

Taking notes on an interview

Before you interview someone, write your interview questions on a piece of paper. Leave room below each question for notes about the speaker's answers. Don't write complete sentences for the answers. Write only the most important words.

Read this sample from an interview.

> **Q:** What are your favorite foods?
>
> **A:** Well, I like pizza a lot. I also really like teriyaki chicken. Cherries are my favorite fruit.
>
> **Q:** What foods do you eat every day?
>
> **A:** Let's see. I eat yogurt every morning for breakfast. I also have rice with my dinner every day. Sometimes I have rice at lunchtime, too.

Look at the sample notes below. Notice the note-taker left room for notes about the speaker's answers and wrote only the most important words.

Q:	What are your favorite foods?
A:	pizza, teriyaki chicken, cherries
Q:	What foods do you eat every day?
A:	yogurt, rice

B. ORGANIZE IDEAS Work with your partner and prepare your survey.

1. Look at your ten questions from Activity A. Circle your four best questions. Include at least one opinion question.

2. Write your questions. Leave room for notes about the speaker's answers.

iQ PRACTICE Go online for more practice with taking notes on an interview. *Practice > Unit 3 > Activity 11*

When you are answering an interviewer's questions, remember to use the phrases *In my opinion* and *I think that* to give your opinion and then give a reason. Review the Speaking Skill box in Unit 2 on page 35 and the Critical Thinking Strategy on page 36.

TIP FOR SUCCESS

When you want more information, you can ask a **follow-up question**. For example: *Why is it your favorite? Why not?*

C. SPEAK Follow these steps. Look at the Self-Assessment checklist below before you begin.

1. Each partner works individually. Use the questions to interview another student in your class. Take notes on his or her answers.

2. Look over your notes. Are they clear? Make changes and add words to make your notes clearer.

3. Work with your partner. Check your notes. Did you write the student's answers correctly?

4. Compare your answers with your partner's answers. How are the answers the same or different? Share your ideas with the class.

iQ PRACTICE Go online for your alternate Unit Assignment.
Practice > Unit 3 > Activity 12

CHECK AND REFLECT

A. CHECK Think about the Unit Assignment as you complete the Self-Assessment checklist.

SELF-ASSESSMENT	Yes	No
Our interview questions were clear.	☐	☐
I used vocabulary from this unit.	☐	☐
I used gerunds and infinitives correctly.	☐	☐
I gave reasons for my opinions when answering questions.	☐	☐

B. REFLECT Discuss these questions with a partner or group.

1. What is something new you learned in this unit?

2. Think about the Unit Question—How do you choose your food? Is your answer different now than when you started this unit? If yes, how is it different? Why?

iQ PRACTICE Go to the online discussion board to discuss these questions.
Practice > Unit 3 > Activity 13

TRACK YOUR SUCCESS

iQ PRACTICE Go online to check the words and phrases you have learned in this unit. *Practice > Unit 3 > Activity 14*

Check (✓) the skills you learned. If you need more work on a skill, refer to the page(s) in parentheses.

LISTENING	☐ I can listen for reasons. (p. 44)
CRITICAL THINKING	☐ I can understand causes and effects. (p. 46)
VOCABULARY	☐ I can use prefixes and suffixes. (p. 48)
PRONUNCIATION	☐ I can recognize stressed syllables. (p. 49)
GRAMMAR	☐ I can use verbs + gerunds or infinitives correctly. (p. 52)
NOTE-TAKING	☐ I can take notes during an interview. (p. 55)
SPEAKING	☐ I can give an opinion. (p. 56)
OBJECTIVE ▶	☐ I can use information and ideas to design a survey and interview a classmate.

Sociology

4

What do you enjoy doing?

A. Discuss these questions with your classmates.

1. Complete the chart. Then compare charts with a partner.

What is . . .	
a fun activity?	
a boring activity?	
an exciting activity?	
a dangerous activity?	
an interesting activity?	

2. Look at the photo. Describe what the person is doing. Why do people do this?

B. Listen to *The Q Classroom* online. Then answer these questions.

1. What did the students say? What are some things they like to do?

2. Do you like the same things that they like?

iQ PRACTICE Go to the online discussion board to discuss the Unit Question with your classmates. *Practice > Unit 4 > Activity 1*

UNIT OBJECTIVE

Listen to a classroom discussion. Use information and ideas to have a group discussion about fun places in your area.

Remember: In conversations, speakers give reasons to explain their activities. They often ask for reasons with **why**. They use words like **because** and **because of** to show they are giving a reason. After *because*, use a complete sentence. After *because of*, use a noun or noun phrase.

> A: **Why** do you go to the mall?
> B: I go to the mall **because** <u>there are a lot of great shops</u>!
>   I go to the mall **because of** <u>the great shops</u>!

Use a T-chart to take notes about activities and reasons. The T-chart below shows an activity and a reason for the example sentences above. A T-chart can help you organize your ideas.

Activity	Reason
go to the mall	a lot of great shops

ANALYZE Listen to two students talking in a shopping mall. Then complete the T-chart below with reasons.

Activity	Reasons
the man comes to the mall	1. <u>to buy clothes</u> 2. _____ 3. _____ 4. _____
the woman comes to the mall	5. _____ 6. _____

iQ PRACTICE Go online for more practice with taking notes on reasons.
Practice > Unit 4 > Activity 2

LISTENING

OBJECTIVE ▶

Free-Time Activities

You are going to listen to a class discussion about free-time activities. Think about what you enjoy doing.

playing a board game

PREVIEW THE LISTENING

VOCABULARY SKILL REVIEW

In Unit 2, you learned about using the dictionary to find antonyms. Can you find antonyms for the vocabulary words *modern*, *outdoors*, *crowded*, and *relaxing*?

ACADEMIC LANGUAGE

The word **nature** is very common in both spoken and written academic English. It is frequently part of the phrase **the nature of**. For example, *It is the nature of children to question their parents.*

─────── **OPAL**
Oxford Phrasal Academic Lexicon

A. VOCABULARY Here are some words from the listening. Read the sentences. Then write each underlined word in the correct sentence below.

a. Anna's new house is very <u>modern</u>. It has all the newest technology.

b. From here, we can see the busy market <u>scene</u> below.

c. Picking apples in the fall is a family <u>tradition</u>.

d. In the summer, we sometimes eat <u>outdoors</u>. It's nice to be outside.

e. The tall trees <u>provide</u> shade in the park.

f. Sun-Hee likes to be in <u>nature</u>. She loves trees and flowers.

g. James doesn't like <u>crowded</u> places. There are too many people!

h. Keith likes to read on the weekend. It's very <u>relaxing</u>.

1. I like to sit by the lake in the evening. It's _____.

2. I don't like _____ cars. I like older cars.

3. There are a lot of people here! It's really _____.

4. Some companies _____ free meals for their workers.

5. I love to spend time in _____. I like to look at the trees, the grass, and the animals.

6. The police came to the _____ of the accident.

7. I like to play basketball _____. I don't like to play in a gym.

8. In some countries, it is a _____ to eat special foods on New Year's Day.

iQ PRACTICE Go online for more practice with the vocabulary.
Practice > Unit 4 > Activities 3–4

B. PREVIEW You are going to listen to a discussion about board games and other free-time activities. What do you think the speakers will say about board games? Check (✓) your ideas.

☐ 1. Board games are fun.

☐ 2. People are buying more games.

☐ 3. It can be stressful to play board games when people want to win too much.

☐ 4. People used to play board games, but they don't anymore.

☐ 5. Playing games is relaxing.

☐ 6. Board games are boring.

WORK WITH THE LISTENING

A. CATEGORIZE Read the sentences. Then listen to the discussion. Write *T* (true), *F* (false), or *N* (not enough information).

iQ RESOURCES Go online to download extra vocabulary support.
Resources > Extra Vocabulary > Unit 4

____ 1. The discussion is mostly about video games.

____ 2. All of the speakers are students.

____ 3. The discussion is part of a sociology class.

____ 4. All the speakers have a good opinion of board games.

____ 5. The speakers discuss opinions but not facts.

B. IDENTIFY Listen again. Circle the correct answer.

1. The group are talking about free-time activities you can only do ____.

    a. on weekends   b. with your friends and family   c. without a computer or phone

2. Miyumi says that when her brothers are not on their computers, they usually spend time ____.

   a. with their family   b. by themselves   c. outdoors in nature

3. Abdel says that sometimes his friends and family ____.

   a. are too competitive   b. don't care about games   c. like to relax together

4. Miyumi says that free-time activities have different kinds of effects. The effects can depend on ____.

   a. the activity you do   b. the person   c. the time of day

5. Hector says that he ____.

   a. doesn't like board games   b. enjoys walking outdoors   c. always likes being with people

6. Christine says that spending time ____ is very important in today's modern world.

   a. in nature   b. in the city   c. on your computer

SKILL REVIEW Listening for reasons

Remember: In conversations, speakers often use **why** to ask for reasons. They use **because** to give reasons. Review the Listening Skill box in Unit 3 on page 44.

C. ANALYZE Listen again. Take notes in the chart.

Activity	Reasons
Sales of board games have been going up.	People like to get together ____ ____.
Christine plays board games.	She likes to ² ____.
Gia plays board games.	It's ³ ____ ____ and ____. They make her ⁴ ____.
Abdel thinks board games are stressful.	Sometimes people want to ⁵ ____.
Hector likes to spend time alone.	He thinks it can be ⁶ ____.

iQ PRACTICE Go online for additional listening and comprehension.
Practice ⟩ Unit 4 ⟩ Activity 5

CRITICAL THINKING STRATEGY

Noticing differences

When you hear information about more than one thing or person, some information may be different. Listen for words that show differences. Words like *but*, *while*, and *however* introduce differences. Antonyms can also show differences.

Information	Differences
Uma likes to go to museums, **but** Kayla doesn't like museums at all.	Uma and Kayla are different in the way they feel about museums. (Uma's feelings ≠ Kayla's feelings)
Ben thinks lectures are **interesting**. He thinks sports are **boring**.	For Ben, lectures are interesting and sports are boring. *Interesting* and *boring* are antonyms. (Ben's opinion of lectures ≠ Ben's opinion of sports)

iQ PRACTICE Go online to watch the Critical Thinking Video and check your comprehension. *Practice > Unit 4 > Activity 6*

D. APPLY Listen again. Complete the sentences about differences.

1. _____ thinks board games are _____, but Abdel thinks they are _____.

2. _____ and _____ like to spend time with friends and family, but _____ likes to spend time alone.

3. Gia likes games, but _____ gets mad if she doesn't win.

4. Walking in _____ is less stressful than walking _____.

walking in a park

walking on crowded city streets

E. CREATE Reread sentences 1–3 in Activity D. What are *your* opinions and preferences? Rewrite the sentences with your own information to express differences between you and the people in the listening.

I think board games are fun, but Abdel thinks they are stressful.

1. _____

_____

2. _____

_____

3. _____

_____

F. DISCUSS Work with a partner. Look at Preview the Listening Activity B on page 62. Which statements express ideas that are very different or almost opposite in meaning?

BUILDING VOCABULARY Collocations with *do, play,* and *go*

Words for activities often follow the verbs *do, play,* and *go*.

> They **do gymnastics** on Saturdays.
> She **plays basketball** at her school.
> He **goes skiing** in the mountains.

do	play	go*
do aerobics	play baseball	go hiking
do crosswords	play Scrabble	go jogging
do gymnastics	play soccer	go shopping
do judo	play tennis	go skiing
do nothing	play video games	go swimming

*You usually use the verb *go* with a gerund (verb + *-ing*).

TIP FOR SUCCESS

The word *let's* introduces suggestions.

A. APPLY Complete the conversations with *play, do,* or *go.*

1. **Sara:** Emma, I'm bored. Let's do something.

   Emma: Sure. Let's _____ shopping.

   Sara: I don't like shopping. Let's _____ video games.

   Emma: No, I'm not good at video games. Uh, do you want to _____ hiking?

   Sara: OK. That's a great idea!

2. **John:** Mike, I want to lose weight. What do you do for exercise?

   Mike: I _____ judo. I have a class twice a week.

   John: Do you still _____ gymnastics?

   Mike: No, it was too difficult.

judo   skiing

3. **Sandra:** Mei, do you want to _____ swimming with me?

   Mei: No, thanks. I have training.

   Sandra: Oh, do you _____ a sport?

   Mei: Yes, I _____ soccer. Hey, do you want to _____ skiing this weekend?

   Sandra: Sure, that sounds like fun!

B. CREATE Answer the questions with information about yourself. Use *play*, *do*, or *go*. Then ask and answer the questions with a partner.

1. A: What do you like to do on weekends?

   B: I like to _____.

2. A: What do you like to do at night?

   B: I like to _____.

3. A: What else do you like to do for fun?

   B: I like to _____.

4. A: What do you hate to do?

   B: I really hate to _____.

iQ PRACTICE Go online for more practice with collocations with *do, play,* and *go.*
Practice > Unit 4 > Activity 7

WORK WITH THE VIDEO

A. PREVIEW Do you enjoy making art? Why? Why not?

VIDEO VOCABULARY

artist (n.) a person who makes art, like paintings

clay (n.) a type of sticky dirt that you can use to make bricks or pots

creativity (n.) the use of imagination or new ideas to make something

tile (n.) a thin square of clay or metal

decorate (v.) to make something more attractive by adding to it

a potter making a pot

iQ RESOURCES Go online to watch the video about a pottery competition. *Resources › Video › Unit 4 › Unit Video*

B. IDENTIFY Watch the video two or three times. Circle the correct answer.

1. The artists are working on ____.

   a. pots   b. tiles   c. paintings

2. They need to decorate ____ of them.

   a. nine   b. ninety   c. ninety-nine

3. Some artists think their neighbors' ideas might be ____.

   a. the same   b. better   c. worse

4. Some artists are excited because there are many different ____.

   a. competitions   b. winners   c. patterns

5. The ____ look at the artists' work.

   a. judges   b. potters   c. neighbors

6. One way the artists do NOT show creativity is with ____.

   a. the difficulty b. unusual ideas   c. the order they use

C. EXTEND Would you like to be in a competition like this? Why or why not?

SAY WHAT YOU THINK

A. IDENTIFY Think about the listening and the unit video. Give your opinion about fun. Circle *Yes* or *No* for each sentence. Then compare ideas with a partner.

WHAT MAKES SOMETHING FUN?

1.	Fun activities teach you something.	Yes	No
2.	Fun activities are always active.	Yes	No
3.	Dangerous activities are sometimes fun.	Yes	No
4.	Relaxing activities are not fun.	Yes	No
5.	You need to be with other people to have fun.	Yes	No
6.	It's fun to spend time in nature.	Yes	No
7.	Making something is fun.	Yes	No
8.	It's fun to win.	Yes	No

B. DISCUSS Discuss the questions.

1. What is your favorite activity? Why is it your favorite?

2. Where do you go to do things you enjoy?

SPEAKING

OBJECTIVE ▶

At the end of this unit, you are going to have a group discussion about things you enjoy doing in your area.

GRAMMAR Subject and object pronouns

1. Subjects and objects can be nouns.
   - Subjects come before verbs in statements.
   - Objects come after verbs or prepositions like *at, in,* and *on.*

subject	verb	object	preposition + object
Kate	likes	the **book.**	
My **brother**	runs	—	in the **park.**

2. Pronouns replace nouns.
   - You use some pronouns for subjects.
   - You use other pronouns for objects.

	subject pronoun	object pronoun
singular	**I** have a great soccer coach.	He helps **me.**
	You are good at swimming.	I want to go with **you.**
	He goes hiking a lot.	I sometimes see **him** in the park.
	She is good at math.	I like studying with **her.**
	I like the park. **It's** really big.	My friends like **it,** too.
plural	**We** go shopping on Sundays.	Our friends meet **us** at the mall.
	You play baseball a lot.	I sometimes see you at the field.
	They are great soccer players.	I like to watch **them.**

3. You usually use the pronouns *he / him, she / her, it / it, we / us,* and *they / them* after you know the noun.

Mary has a brother named Tom. **She** studies with **him** every Friday.

(Mary = **She**; Tom = **him**)

iQ RESOURCES Go online to watch the Grammar Skill Video.
Resources > Video > Unit 4 > Grammar Skill Video

A. IDENTIFY Circle the correct pronoun.

1. (He / Him) goes hiking on Saturdays.

2. Let's go to the mall with (they / them) tomorrow.

3. (We / Us) like to spend time at the park.

4. Sarah's friends make (she / her) laugh.

5. I like this art. (He / It) is beautiful.

6. John and (I / me) love to play tennis.

7. James plays baseball with Sam and (I / me).

8. Fun activities sometimes teach (we / us) something.

B. APPLY Complete each sentence with a pronoun for the underlined word.

1. That TV <u>show</u> is really exciting. I watch _____ every week.

2. Isabel's <u>sister</u> loves to go hiking. _____ goes every weekend.

3. Family <u>traditions</u> are important. I really appreciate _____.

4. I see my <u>grandmother</u> on Wednesdays. I have lunch with _____.

5. My <u>classes</u> are very interesting, but _____ are difficult.

6. <u>Faisal and Miteb</u> go jogging in the park. Then _____ have lunch.

7. <u>We</u> play basketball in the gym. Sometimes our friends join _____.

8. I want to play tennis with <u>you</u>. _____ are an excellent player.

jogging in the park

C. ANALYZE Look back at Activities A and B. Write an *S* over all the subject pronouns. Write an *O* over all the object pronouns.

D. APPLY Complete the conversation with the correct subject and object pronouns.

Sarah: Maria, how do _____ like your cooking class?

1

Maria: I love _____! My teacher is great. She's from France,

2

and _____ really knows how to cook. What's new with you?

3

Sarah: I'm taking a writing class.

Maria: Oh, do _____ write stories?

4

Sarah: No, _____ write poetry. The class is really fun.

5

I like the other students. _____ are very talented.

6

Maria: That's great. Hey, my friends and I are going to the beach this weekend. Do _____ want to come with _____?
7   8

Sarah: Sure, that sounds fun and relaxing.

iQ PRACTICE Go online for more practice with subject and object pronouns.
Practice > Unit 4 > Activity 8

iQ PRACTICE Go online for the Grammar Expansion: possessive adjectives.
Practice > Unit 4 > Activity 9

PRONUNCIATION Reduced pronouns

You usually say pronouns quickly, with no stress. When you say *he, him, her,* and *them,* you don't usually pronounce the beginning sounds. You "**reduce**" the words.

| I think **he**'s at the park. | I don't see **him**. |
| Is that **her** bike? | Let's call **them**. |

You <u>do</u> pronounce the "h" of *he* when it's the first word in a sentence.

He's at the park.

A. APPLY Complete the conversations with *he, him, her,* and *them*. Then listen and check your answers. Practice the conversations with a partner. Say the reduced forms.

1. A: John is a fun guy. How do you know _____? Does _____ play soccer with you?

   B: No, I know _____ from school. How do you know _____?

   A: _____ spends time at the park near my house. Sometimes _____ plays basketball there with my friends and me.

2. A: Anna's sister Emma is here this weekend. Do you know _____?

   B: Yes, I do. I really like _____.

   A: Me too. Do you think Anna and Emma want to go for a walk with us this afternoon?

   B: Maybe. Let's call _____.

B. COMPOSE Write four sentences with *he, him, her,* and *them*. Then take turns reading your sentences with a partner.

iQ PRACTICE Go online for more practice with reduced pronouns.
Practice > Unit 4 > Activity 10

Use these expressions to **agree** with another person's opinion.

Agreeing with a positive opinion	Agreeing with a negative opinion
A: I like swimming.	A: I don't like swimming.
B: **I do too. / Me too.***	B: **I don't either. / Me neither.***

* *Me too* and *Me neither* sound more informal.

Use these expressions to **disagree** with another person's opinion.
These expressions sound more friendly or polite.

Disagreeing politely	
A: I think that the building is pretty.	A: I love that park. How about you?
B: **Oh, I don't know.**	B: **I'm not sure.**

I do too.   I'm not sure.

A. IDENTIFY Listen to the short conversations. Check (✓) *Agree* or *Disagree* for each conversation. Then listen again and write the expression that you hear.

	Agree	Disagree	Expression
1.	☐	☐	
2.	☐	☐	
3.	☐	☐	
4.	☐	☐	
5.	☐	☐	
6.	☐	☐	

B. CREATE Write six sentences about things that you like or don't like. Then read them to a partner. Your partner will agree or disagree.

1. I really like _____.

2. I don't like _____.

3. I think _____.

4. I think _____.

5. I enjoy _____.

6. I hate _____.

iQ PRACTICE   Go online for more practice with agreeing and disagreeing.
Practice > Unit 4 > Activity 11

UNIT ASSIGNMENT
OBJECTIVE ▶ **Have a group discussion about things you enjoy doing in your area**

In this assignment, you are going to have a group discussion about the "top five" enjoyable things to do in your area. Think about the unit question, "What do you enjoy doing?" Use the listening, the unit video, and your work in this unit. Look at the Self-Assessment checklist on page 74.

CONSIDER THE IDEAS

A. IDENTIFY Listen to a group discuss activities and places they enjoy in their area. What activities do they talk about? Check (✓) the activities. Then compare with a partner.

☐ hiking   ☐ reading books   ☐ taking dance classes

☐ playing tennis   ☐ going to plays   ☐ taking computer classes

☐ playing soccer   ☐ going to a museum   ☐ lying on the beach

☐ going to the gym   ☐ going to concerts   ☐ playing video games

B. EXTEND Do you agree with the answers in Activity A? Do you enjoy those activities? Which activities do you enjoy? Discuss your answers with a partner.

PREPARE AND SPEAK

A. FIND IDEAS What are your five favorite things to do in your area? Complete the chart with your ideas. Give reasons for each place.

Name of activity	Where do you do it?	Why do you enjoy it?
1.		
2.		
3.		
4.		
5.		

TIP FOR SUCCESS

You can share ideas and give suggestions with the expressions *How about . . . ?* and *What about . . . ?*

B. ORGANIZE IDEAS Choose three ideas from Activity A. Practice different ways to share your ideas. You can use these phrases.

I think that hiking is enjoyable because it's good exercise and it's outdoors.

How about hiking? It lets you get out in nature.

C. SPEAK Work with a group. Discuss your ideas. Look at the Self-Assessment checklist below before you begin.

- Share your three activities and your reasons.
- Listen carefully to others' ideas. Agree or disagree with them.
- As a group, choose the best five activities.

iQ PRACTICE   Go online for your alternate Unit Assignment.
Practice > Unit 4 > Activity 12

CHECK AND REFLECT

A. CHECK Think about the Unit Assignment as you complete the Self-Assessment checklist.

SELF-ASSESSMENT	Yes	No
My information was clear.	☐	☐
I used vocabulary from this unit.	☐	☐
I made notes using a T-chart.	☐	☐
I used subject and object pronouns correctly.	☐	☐
I used expressions for agreeing and disagreeing.	☐	☐
I used reduced words correctly.	☐	☐

B. REFLECT Discuss these questions with a partner or group.

1. What is something new you learned in this unit?
2. Think about the Unit Question—What do you enjoy doing? Is your answer different now than when you started this unit? If yes, how is it different? Why?

iQ PRACTICE   Go to the online discussion board to discuss these questions.
Practice > Unit 4 > Activity 13

74   UNIT 4   What do you enjoy doing?

TRACK YOUR SUCCESS

iQ PRACTICE Go online to check the words and phrases you have learned in this unit. *Practice > Unit 4 > Activity 14*

Check (✓) the skills you learned. If you need more work on a skill, refer to the page(s) in parentheses.

NOTE-TAKING	☐ I can take notes on reasons. (p. 60)
LISTENING	☐ I can listen for reasons. (p. 63)
CRITICAL THINKING	☐ I can notice differences. (p. 64)
VOCABULARY	☐ I can understand collocations with *do*, *play*, and *go*. (p. 65)
GRAMMAR	☐ I can use subject and object pronouns correctly. (p. 69)
PRONUNCIATION	☐ I can reduce the pronouns *he*, *him*, *her*, and *them*. (p. 71)
SPEAKING	☐ I can agree and disagree. (p. 72)

OBJECTIVE ▶   ☐ I can use information and ideas to have a group discussion about fun places in my area.

🔑 The **Oxford 3000**™ is a list of the 3,000 core words that every learner of English needs to know. The words have been chosen based on their frequency in the Oxford English Corpus and relevance to learners of English. Every word is aligned to the CEFR, guiding learners on the words they should know at the A1–B2 level.

OPAL The **Oxford Phrasal Academic Lexicon** is an essential guide to the most important words and phrases to know for academic English. The word lists are based on the Oxford Corpus of Academic English and the British Academic Spoken English corpus.

The **Common European Framework of Reference for Language (CEFR)** provides a basic description of what language learners have to do to use language effectively. The system contains 6 reference levels: A1, A2, B1, B2, C1, C2.

UNIT 1
belong to *(v. phr.)* 🔑 A2
club *(n.)* 🔑 A1
collect *(v.)* 🔑 A2
good at *(phr.)* 🔑 A1
hobbies *(n.)* 🔑 A1
interested in *(phr.)* 🔑 OPAL A1
team *(n.)* 🔑 A1

UNIT 2
campus *(n.)* 🔑 B1
community *(n.)* 🔑 OPAL A2
download *(v.)* 🔑 A2
foreign language *(n. phr.)* 🔑 A2
online *(adj., adv.)* 🔑 OPAL A1
professor *(n.)* 🔑 A2
skill *(n.)* 🔑 OPAL A1
special *(adj.)* 🔑 A1

UNIT 3
avoid *(v.)* 🔑 OPAL A2
flavor *(n.)* 🔑 B2
ingredient *(n.)* 🔑 B1
memory *(n.)* 🔑 A2
nutritious *(adj.)*
organic *(adj.)* B2
vegetarian *(n.)*

UNIT 4
crowded *(adj.)* 🔑 A2
modern *(adj.)* 🔑 OPAL A1
nature *(n.)* 🔑 OPAL A2
outdoors *(n.)* 🔑 B1
provide *(v.)* 🔑 OPAL A2
relaxing *(adj.)* 🔑 B1
scene *(n.)* 🔑 A2
tradition *(n.)* 🔑 A2

UNIT 5
affordable *(adj.)* B2
comfortable *(adj.)* 🔑 A2
condition *(n.)* 🔑 OPAL A2
demand *(n.)* 🔑 OPAL B2
entertainment *(n.)* 🔑 B1
housing *(n.)* 🔑 B2
increase *(v.)* 🔑 OPAL A2
landlord *(n.)* C1
location *(n.)* 🔑 OPAL B1
noisy *(adj.)* 🔑 A2
private *(adj.)* 🔑 OPAL B1
problem *(n.)* 🔑 OPAL A1
public transportation *(n. phr.)* A2
rent *(n.)* 🔑 B1
roommate *(n.)*
shortage *(n.)* B2

UNIT 6

control *(n.)* ♟ OPAL **A2**
depends on *(v. phr.)* ♟ OPAL **A2**
diet *(n.)* ♟ **A1**
energy *(n.)* ♟ OPAL **A2**
exercise *(v.)* ♟ OPAL **A1**
healthy *(adj.)* ♟ **A1**
lonely *(adj.)* ♟ **B1**
manage *(v.)* ♟ **A2**
pill *(n.)* **B2**
produce *(v.)* ♟ OPAL **A2**
reduce *(v.)* ♟ OPAL **A2**
run-down *(adj.)*
stress *(n.)* ♟ OPAL **A2**
vitamin *(n.)* ♟ **B2**

UNIT 7

advantage *(n.)* ♟ OPAL **A2**
average *(adj.)* ♟ OPAL **A2**
climate *(n.)* ♟ OPAL **A2**
culture *(n.)* ♟ OPAL **A1**
decision *(n.)* ♟ OPAL **A2**
disappointed *(adj.)* ♟ **B1**
either *(adv.)* ♟ **A2**
else *(adv.)* ♟ **A1**
experience *(n.)* ♟ OPAL **A2**
historic *(adj.)* ♟ **B1**
lecture *(n.)* ♟ OPAL **A2**
nervous *(adj.)* ♟ **A2**
recently *(adv.)* ♟ OPAL **A2**
skyscraper *(n.)*
whatever *(pro.)* ♟ OPAL **B1**

UNIT 8

available *(adj.)* ♟ OPAL **A2**
busy *(adj.)* ♟ **A1**
happen *(v.)* ♟ OPAL **A1**
have trouble with *(v. phr.)*
information *(n.)* ♟ OPAL **A1**
just *(adv.)* ♟ **A1**
keep in touch *(v. phr.)*
look up *(v. phr.)*
presentation *(n.)* ♟ OPAL **B1**
shut down *(v. phr.)*
smartphone *(n.)*
text message *(n. phr.)* ♟ **A1**
type *(v.)* ♟ OPAL **B1**
use up *(v. phr.)* ♟ **A1**
work on *(v. phr.)* **A1**